CRAPS
for the
CLUELESS

CRAPS
for the
CLUELESS

◆

A BEGINNER'S GUIDE TO PLAYING AND WINNING

John Patrick

LYLE STUART
Kensington Publishing Corp.
www.kensingtonbooks.com

LYLE STUART books are published by

Kensington Publishing Corp.
850 Third Avenue
New York, NY 10022

All Kensington titles, imprints, and distributed lines are available at special quantity discounts for bulk purchases for sales promotions, premiums, fund raising, educational, or institutional use. Special book excerpts or customized printings can also be created to fit specific needs. For details, write or phone the office of the Kensington special sales manager: Kensington Publishing Corp., 850 Third Avenue, New York, NY 10022, attn: Special Sales Department, phone 1-800-221-2647.

Lyle Stuart is a trademark of Kensington Publishing Corp.

First printing 1998

10 9 8 7 6

Printed in the United States of America

Library of Congress Cataloging-in-Publication Data

Patrick, John, 1932–
     Craps for the clueless : a beginner's guide to playing and winning
  / John Patrick.
        p.   cm.
     "A Lyle Stuart book."
     ISBN 0-8184-0599-6 (pbk.)
     1. Craps (Game)   I. Title
  GV1303.P37   1998
  795.1′2—dc21   98-22808
                                                           CIP

To my mother and father
and to my daughters, Lori and Colleen,
the most important people in my life

CONTENTS

PREFACE

Did you see the title of this book? It reads *Craps for the Clueless,* and that's because it's a book dedicated to a beginner's look at this very popular game. We explain the whole game, the layout, the vigorish, the odds, and all of that nonsense that people think is so important in gambling. Then we get into the real meat of craps, which is money management and discipline. There are systems, methods, and rules to follow that help you become a consistent winner at this game. The main part of gambling is controlling losses, which is called loss limits. This is pounded home in detail.

Will you listen to these suggestions? I dunno, but if you wanna become a consistent winner, you best follow these simple rules. It's called learning how to win.

The book may be titled *Craps for the Clueless,* but in reality, it's for everyone who plays craps.

CRAPS
for the
CLUELESS

1

Introduction:
The Game of Craps

You ever play craps before? You ever go to a casino, pick up them bones and toss them across the table, thereby igniting a mixed reaction from the players who gather around the table and live and die with every roll? Well, craps is both an easy game to play and is exciting in its multiple assortment of possible wagers.

I've written ten books on gambling, including *Basic Craps* and the greatest gambling book ever written, *Advanced Craps*. The one you are reading now is for beginners, because it goes all the way in explaining things that, although not needed in deciding wins and losses, are necessary in gaining total insight into a great game. Will you learn how to win? You bet your britches you will! Will you pay attention? Let's see.

CRAPS FOR THE CLUELESS

Pretty neat title, ain't it? Well, don't go thinking I was so smart to come up with it, because I didn't. My editor at Carol Publishing,

Allan J. Wilson, is the genius who arrived at that name, and I kind of like it. Beats my own brainstorm-of-a-title: *So You Wanna Be a Gambler,* which describes my previous ten books.

Craps for the Clueless is trying to go way, way, way back to the very essence of what craps is all about. It is aimed at the gambling neophyte who needs to have the game laid out in terms that even a four-year-old could understand.

Don't think for one second that I am saying that the millions of craps players now standing at the tables know everything about the game, because they don't. Sure, they know the object of craps, but they lack the skills of money management and discipline that separate the real players from the dorks.

I'm getting ahead of myself. We'll get to money management and discipline in later chapters. Right now, let's give you an idea of what you'll find on the following pages:

- A complete, basic approach to craps
- Skills to handle your **bankroll**
- All the **knowledge** you need to understand the good and bad plays
- A fabulous (if I do say so myself) **money management** approach
- An awareness of the all-important aspect of **discipline**

It's all coming up in simple explanations in the following chapters. Will you listen? Maybe not, but read on anyway.

THE BIG FOUR

Before we get into the meat of the game, you need to understand what it takes to win consistently. It was already touched on in the previous chapter, but because it is absolutely essential you learn this, we'll go over it again.

There are four things you need in any form of gambling to help you have a shot at winning. I call them the Big Four. These are fundamentally important in increasing your chances of winning. Listed in order, they are:

1. **Bankroll**   This is the amount of money you bring to battle. Every single betting decision spins off of your starting bankroll.
2. **Knowledge of the Game**   You must be perfect in understanding everything about the game you are playing, in this case, craps. This knowledge will help you avoid bad bets and increase your chance of winning by holding down losses.
3. **Money Management**   You'll find oodles of chapters on this subject because it is so crucial to your game. Money management can be summed up by asking yourself the following question: What do I bet after a win and what do I bet after a loss?
4. **Discipline**   This will determine whether you are in a position to gamble sensibly. It takes brains and guts to use discipline at the tables. Let's see if you can qualify on both counts.

This entire book will be broken down into sections, each going over the Big Four. The other two sections will deal with the things you need to help you learn the game of craps, but it all starts with the Big Four.

THE LITTLE THREE

Right in the back of the Big Four is the Little Three. These contain three additional necessities that help in your awareness of the pitfalls of gambling. They are:

1. Theory
2. Logic
3. Trends

Each of these categories gets their own section, so you get to see how they back up the Big Four.

For those of you squirming in your seats, waiting to learn about craps, hold on to your britches. In the chapter, "Knowledge of the Game," you'll get a bellyful of charts and explanations of the entire craps table. Believe it or not, this section is more important than the "Knowledge" chapter because it shows you how to lay out your day, rather than learning about the craps layout.

Sections on the Little Three will follow, but here are other issues and terms you'll become familiar with:

- Loss limits
- Win goals
- Sessions
- Reality
- Series
- Charting

Each of these will be addressed in their own sections, so look for them.

GAMING THEORY

Everybody has an opinion about everything. That's only natural and is the way it should be. I have an opinion on how to correct the problem with the IRS. It is my opinion, or theory, on how to make this system work. Of course, nobody gives a rat's tail what my theory is because I'm not qualified enough or powerful enough to put it to work.

I still have a theory, though, and you probably do too. In fact, we have theories on most everything, including human rights, women's rights, animal rights, big business, government spending, political corruption, crime, immigration, child rearing, and gambling. Just like you, my theories remain in my head, because nobody wants to hear them unless I am an expert on any of these subjects, which I'm not, except gambling.

In that area, I am considered a genius, because I do it for a living and am successful at it. Was I born smart in gambling? Heck, no. I was the biggest dork who ever threw them bones across a blanket in the back alleys of New Jersey, the tables in Las Vegas, Reno, and Tahoe, barrack's floors in various army camps around the world, and the tables on the riverboats that ran illegal games on the Mississippi River.

I lost most of the time until I learned: how to bet, when to quit, and how to cut losses. These theories work, and now people wanna hear them. They are my theories, my opinions on how to gamble at craps. Everybody has theories on gambling, and mine are very conservative. You may not like them, but at least give them a look.

LOGIC

This is the second leg of the Little Three and has to do with your approach to gambling. Anything to do with gambling has a logical explanation:

- In blackjack, you wouldn't stand on hard 16 against the dealer's up-cards of 10, Jack, Queen, or King, because the dealer could turn over a 7, 8, 9, 10, Jack, Queen, King, or Ace and beat you eight ways. The logical move would be to hit the hard 16. Right? Right.
- In baseball, you wouldn't bet against Greg Maddox of the Atlanta Braves, and with a hapless team in last place just because you liked the price. The logical move would be to pass on the game.
- In poker, you wouldn't raise two pair of 10s and 4s against an opponent showing three Queens, regardless of your attempt at bluffing him. The logical move is to fold and wait for the next hand.

These are all logical explanations to obvious situations. Logic comes into play when handling your bankroll and when making your bets at the craps table in areas that give you the least chance of losing. My conservative style deals with logic, and while you may not like it, at least see how this approach cuts losses. My friend, Will Winbigg, wants to win big. He wants to bring home something like $6,000 with a $600 bankroll. It's a nice thought but hardly logical.

What does a professional gambler win with $600? Anything between $40 and $60. Sounds small—but it's logical. The reason people lose at gambling is because they fail to grasp the fact that they are playing a game that offers them only a fifty-fifty shot at winning, regardless of their bankroll or knowledge. So, logically, they should be ecstatic with a 10 or 20 percent return on their money. Doubling and tripling your bankroll at a fifty-fifty game is illogical. I'm sure you'll eventually realize that.

TRENDS

Finally, and most importantly, we come to trends—by far the most significant part of the Little Three. In gambling, trends dominate. There is no way to explain it, but it is clear as a bell that whatever happened before tends to happen again, rather than the other way around. It is not unusual to see fourteen, fifteen, sixteen banks in a row appear in baccarat, then see eleven players' decisions pop up consecutively. That's trends!

In roulette, you've seen that little weightless ball bang out six black numbers in a row. The poor sap who thinks red will show up by virtue of seeing six blacks in a row will wind up betting his next-born, just because he wagered on something he thought was due to occur. He's wrong. Follow that trend!

You gotta learn to read those trends and take advantage of them, because they're gonna happen. We'll go over trends in craps, because it ain't unusual to see a table where every single shooter pops out fourteen place numbers and makes five points in a row while two tables away, the dice are so cold that no shooter has made a point in three days—and yes, there are dingdongs at that game, putting their money on the table, betting the next shooter will crack the North American record for points thrown by one shooter. They think the dice are due to get hot. They'll blow a lot of money waiting.

To illustrate my point, take a coin and flip it one hundred times, keeping a written record of each flip. It ain't gonna be heads, tails, heads, tails, heads, tails all the time. You're gonna see, for example, five heads, six tails, three heads, nine tails, and so forth, and you'll wonder why these streaks occur. I dunno. I can't explain it, but it will happen, just like a blackjack dealer draws 20 or 21 eight straight hands and then breaks her next thirteen hands. It's called streaks or trends, and you must learn when to leave a table when these streaks are going against you. If I could explain why streaks happen, I could also explain why:

- women are smarter than men
- a tree doesn't make a noise when it falls in the forest when nobody is around
- politicians lie
- the check is *not* in the mail
- several other phenomena

I don't know why trends occur, but take my word, they do. When you realize this, you'll zero in on following them. Trends are a big part of your game, believe me!

That about wraps up our look at the basics of gambling. If you don't think these messages are important, then you have a lot in common with my friend, I. M. Madork. That dork thinks that gambling in general and craps in particular is a game where you can win a ton of money, just because you know the object of the game and are bound to break the bank at some casino.

That's a lot of g-a-r-b-a-g-e. You will never get me to tell you that gambling is gonna kick off big returns for your bank account and that if you'll just listen to me you'll be rolling in the dough. Baloney! The reality is that, while craps is an excellent game, you still have to know what to bet after a win and what to bet after a loss. That's what I will show you, but of course, only about 5 percent of you will accept this theory of grinding out small, consistent returns.

As I said in the beginning, the title of this book may seem like it's aimed at the complete novice, but people like my friend N. DeDark is still in the dark about this whole game, even though he's been playing craps for nine years. For your own sake, breeze back through the previous sections, especially those on the Big Four and trends. You'll see their importance as soon as we get to the chapter "Knowledge of the Game," where you can learn about craps and *how* and *why* to apply that knowledge. The next section kicks off the first part of the Big Four: bankroll. Is bankroll important in gambling? Is an engine important in a car?

2

Bankroll

This is the first part of the Big Four and the thing that kicks off your day. Bankroll is the amount of money you bring to the casinos, and every monetary decision you make is based on your bankroll.

Don't go thinking that bankroll necessarily means $8,000, or some other high amount of capital that may be out of your reach. Bankroll is the amount of money that you have, and that could be from $100 to $500. With that bankroll, you will set two immensely important figures: win goals and loss limits.

1. **Win Goals** An intelligent amount of anticipated profit, based on your bankroll.
2. **Loss Limits** An intelligent percentage set against your bankroll that prohibits you from being wiped out.

Each of these all-important factors will be developed in a subsequent chapter, so for now, just gear yourself for setting up these guidelines.

My friend, Lee Tilkash, has a little amount of cash set aside to gamble with and is restricted to a $200 bankroll. No problem. All of her decisions will be set against that figure. She still sets her win goals and loss limits and concentrates on playing only at low-minimum tables. In Atlantic City and on many riverboats, that would be a $5 table. In Las Vegas, she will find $2 and $3 tables and even $1 craps tables. That keeps her in the game and allows her to bet within her means.

On the other hand, my friend Lotta Muny has a lot of money and brings $3,000 as her bankroll. No problem. She can play at high-minimum tables, but (and I mean but) she still must abide by win goals and loss limits, the same as Lee Tilkash and all of the others who have smaller stakes. The percentage of wins and losses stays the same. The only thing that differs is the actual dollar amounts.

Okay, you got the drift. Your bankroll is the amount of money you personally take to the casino—or have I said that before?

SESSIONS

You're heading to the casino with your bankroll safely tucked away in your pocket, with visions of big returns dancing in your head, unaware that your chances of winning are at best fifty-fifty, even if you are a perfect player. You enter the casino and bring out your bankroll. For the sake of example, we'll say half of you have $300 and the other half, $600.

You wanna make sure you don't blow the whole wad at the first table, so you break your bankroll into sessions (or tables). Craps is your game this day, and you decide to test your skills at three different tables. With the $300 bankroll, you divide it into three sessions of $100 each, or $200 per session with the $600 bankroll. It all depends on your stake, divided into equal sessions (tables).

As an option, you could divide your bankroll into four different sessions of equal amounts, which gives the $300 players four sessions at $75 each, and the $600 players four sessions of $150 each. The purpose is to give you different tables to attack, all with equal amounts of buy-ins. You will still set your win goals and loss limits at each table based on what your starting session may be. The amount of your bankroll is not important, although the more you bring, the more flexibility you have and the more sessions you can play.

Do you ever see clowns take their entire bankroll to the first table and bet as if their chips had a disease they want to spread all over the table? A few hours later, they're down to betting $1 hard ways because they caught a cold table. Don't take your entire bankroll to a table! Learn about sessions, because they help you cut losses.

BUY-IN AND SERIES

I can cover these two subjects in one section because the explanations are so simple you'll grasp their meaning in a flash. My friend, Watt E. Cey, is screaming, "What did he say?" because he's not paying attention. He's still trying to figure out the difference between a bankroll and a session.

Buy-in   The amount of money you go up to a table with. It is a session that is a portion of your bankroll. When you go up to the craps table, merely drop your cash on the table right in front of you. That money is called your buy-In.

You are "buying in" with your session money, and you have already set your win goal and loss limit. The buy-in is completed when the dealer, on your side of the table, takes that money and slides it over to the box man, who counts it and announces to your dealer how much it is. We'll say it's $150.

The dealer will give you white, red, and green chips equaling that amount of money. For our $150, the chips may be broken down into the following: ten white ($1) chips, eighteen red ($5) chips, and two green ($25) chips. You take the chips (your buy-in) and place them on the rack in front of you. That completes your buy-in.

You're now ready to get involved in the game, so you place a bet on the pass line. This starts a series of bets you will make for this shooter, so we call it a series.

Series The first bet you make to start a game. That Series continues until the shooter "sevens out" and you lose that Series. The next bet you make on a new game begins another Series.

A quick review:

- Bankroll: The money you take to a casino.
- Session: The money you bring to a table after you divide your bankroll into equal amounts (your decision as to how big or small).
- Buy-in: The amount for that session (see above) you drop on the table that the dealer converts into chips.
- Series: The first bet you make begins a series of bets you will make on that shooter. A series ends when that shooter "sevens-out," or you ask for the dealer to take your bets off. (No further action for that game.)

Got it? It's all very simple and a logical way to start your day.

MINIMUM TABLES

You must grasp what this means. It has to do with the lowest amount you can bet at a table. These minimums are posted at each craps table and are printed on color-coded cards. They are not easy to miss. Most casinos use the following color scheme, but there will always be instances when a casino will deviate and use other colors. Here are the basic schemes:

White: $2 minimum table.
Red: $5 minimum table.
Yellow: $10 minimum table.
Green: $25 minimum table.
Black: $100 minimum table.

Each of these tables also has a maximum bet allowed, unless, of course, you are a high roller and the max is waived. The most popular tables are the $5 ones, which are usually crowded, especially on weekends and holidays, when players try to get involved in these lower minimum tables. Remember, your bankroll will determine the amount of your session and how many sessions you will play. With a $300 bankroll, you have only two choices: three sessions at $100 each or four sessions at $75 each.

My friend, E. Gotrip, is on a perpetual ego trip. His bankroll is $200, but his ego is in the thousands. He wants to play with the high-stakes players, always searching for their acceptance. This dork doesn't realize that they don't give a dingdong for anyone but their own plays. E. Gotrip buys in at a $25 table and realistically has only eight $25 bets to make. At a table going against him, he could be wiped out in two shoots.

Use this as a rule of thumb: take your session money to a table where your first bet is no more than 20 percent of your buy-in. Let's say you start with $150. You make a $5 bet on the pass line with $5 odds. You place the 6 and the 8 for $6 each for a total outlay of $22. That is well within your session amount. You can play comfortably.

Suppose you have $100 for your session. You could play $6 on both the 6 and the 8 and be in line with your percentage. In this case, you have no bet on the pass line. I always go to the lowest minimum table I can find. It allows me to bet small when the dice are going against me, and I can always increase my bets when I get into a winning pattern.

I hope you will also play at the lowest minimum table and stay within 20 percent of your session amount for your first set of bets.

WIN GOALS

I knew you were waiting for this section, licking your chops for the figures that I suggest you shoot for. At the tables, you hear these comments all the time:

"How much did you win?"

"How much can I win?"

"Can I retire with my winnings?"

"I just want to win enough to put my three kids through medical school."

"I'll be happy to triple my money."

"I only wanna double my money. I could live with that."

Those are six statements that you have either said or heard someone say, and they rank right up there (or down there) with dumb statements. You probably don't wanna hear what a professional gambler shoots for, but I gotta tell you anyway: it's 10 percent of the bankroll, and that is on a good day.

I will now pause to allow time for your bubbles to burst, time for you to rant, rave, scream, and curse because you thought your lousy $500 bankroll and the systems I suggest will allow you to live in the lap of luxury forever. Well, keep your day job. That $500 on a good day could kick off a profit of $30 to $50 about 70 percent of the time and a $100 profit about 40 percent to 50 percent of the time. That's a real bonanza!

Okay, time's up. Come back and see the reality of looking for small, consistent returns. Even if you are the best player in the casino, your chances of winning are never better than fifty-fifty.

Look at it another way. Let's say I am the best player in the casino. I have a good, solid bankroll, complete knowledge of the game, fabulous money management moves, and impeccable discipline. Do you know what my chances of winning are? Fifty-fifty. That's it, because the game itself offers only a fifty-fifty chance.

Of course you wanna win big—we all do—but those people who wanna double a $500 bankroll in one day are the same people who put $500 in a 10 percent CD for a year and scream that they are financial geniuses for making $50 on their principal. Then they go to a casino and try to make $500 in one day. It's just not logical.

We'll go over win goals again in the money management section, but for now, start thinking of a 20 percent return as a very good score.

Win goals. Set 'em and abide by 'em.

LOSS LIMITS

This is the most important part of your day—far more important than anything else you will do in the casino. This is the setting of loss limits.

Loss Limits   The amount of money you will allow yourself to lose based on your starting bankroll. Once you reach this limit, you must QUIT. Your loss limits are a percentage of your starting bankroll. Once this percentage is reached, you must QUIT.

Have I made myself perfectly clear? I hope so, because this is the stopgap that prevents you from going belly-up and losing your entire bankroll. The amount of that loss limit should be 50 percent, but you can also set a 40 percent, 30 percent, or even 20 percent limit. This means that once you have lost 50 percent of your starting bankroll, you are done for the day.

Let's say you take $600 to the casino and break it into four sessions of $150 each. Your win goal is 20 percent of that $150, and your loss limit is 50 percent of the $150 you have for each session. Let's also say that on this particular day you're ice cold and reach your loss limit of 50 percent of the $150 at each table. It can happen. That means you're out $75 at each session for a total loss of $300, which is also 50 percent of your starting bankroll of $600.

My friend, I. M. Madork blurts out that if you're only gonna lose a total of $300, why not just take $300 to the casino? Psychologically, my dear Mr. Madork, if you took $300 and lost the whole amount, you would feel awful. You would feel rotten if you got wiped out, but if you brought $600 and lost half of it, you'd still be taking $300 home with you. This scenario, however, is based on you losing. Imagine the scenario with some winnings in your pocket. I can tell you that that would be a pleasant trip back home.

Loss limits are essential, and 50 percent is the ceiling. Personally, I set my loss limits between 20 percent and 30 percent of $500 or more, and while I detest losing, I am bringing home a substantial part of my bankroll. We'll revisit loss limits later, but memorize the following statement and store it in the vast cavern of space that is situated between your ears: "A smart gambler doesn't care how much he wins—he cares about how little he loses."

It's the clueless gambler who sees it the other way around. Enough said.

"SCARED" MONEY

A lot of people play with short bankrolls because of monetary situations, and I ain't condemning them for being in financial disarray, but I am condemning them for playing with short bankrolls, because whenever this is the case, people play "scared." When you play scared, you don't make the proper moves and you end up playing dumb. When you play dumb, you lose, and that is what I'm trying to get you to avoid. I know you think gambling is gonna change your economic situation and put you on Easy Street. You envision walking up to a craps table and being on such a hot roll that you need a wheelbarrow to cart home your winnings.

You have as much chance of striking this gold mine as I have of finding Raquel Welch on my front doorstep. In fact, I have a better chance than you do, and believe me, my chances are slim.

If you're operating with a short bankroll it ain't a sin, but play within that bankroll! If you're gonna play craps and you have $100, divide that into two $50 sessions. Buy in and just play the 6 and 8 (explained fully in the next section). Take either two hits on any combination of the 6 or 8 and take your bets down. Right now, we are talking about you playing with a short bankroll. I would prefer you wait until you can play comfortably, but that's your choice.

My friend, Etch E. Pants, has itchy pants and cannot wait to get to the tables. He has $23 in cash, a roll of dimes, three Indian head pennies, six wooden nickels, and a book of stamps in his pocket. He'll be home early! When you bring a short, or scared, bankroll to a game, it has to make you play with one part of your mind in a panic stage. That's normal. You have two choices:

- Wait until you can play comfortably with a decent bankroll.
- If you insist on playing with a short bankroll, at least play very, very cautiously, and above all, accept very small returns.

The trip home from a casino is very relaxing, even when you win a small amount.

REALITY

This will be the first (but not last) section on reality. It has to do with getting you to realize the reality of entering a casino, sauntering up to a table, and putting your money on them there bones. Craps is a good game, and as you'll see in the next section, it is an easy game to learn.

Before you venture into this world of craps, be aware of the reality of gambling. This is not for the faint of heart. Gambling's popularity has exploded in this country, and the carrot being held out to the patrons of the gambling meccas is the idea that you can change your life with the simple pull of a slot machine handle. Not true!

Yes, someone wins the lottery and someone else occasionally scores a jackpot bonanza, but if you want the reality of the situation, you must understand that more people lose than win. The lives of those people who bet the ranch and lose are most certainly changed—but not for the better!

It is not for me to tell you not to gamble. I only want to make you aware of how tough it is to win the telephone-number amounts that you are led to believe you can win. Here is the reality of gambling. Memorize this. It applies to you:

Seventy percent of the people who enter a casino get ahead. Ninety percent of that 70 percent give the profits back to the house!

This means that out of one hundred people who go to battle, seventy of them have a profit at some point in their day.

Of those seventy people, sixty-three of them give the money back. That should astound you. That should also compel you to think about where you fit into these figures. Are your casino habits reflected in the 70 percent or the 90 percent? Assess your method before turning the page to get a better understanding of what kind of player you are.

The reality? Seven out of one hundred people who gamble have the brains to accept small returns.

WRAPPING UP BANKROLL

We've reached the final leg of the first chapter of the Big Four. There are many issues worth reviewing, but I've picked the following:

- Loss limits
- Reality
- Sessions

Is it very difficult for you to adopt the conservative style of play I have so far outlined? You bet your bottom dollar it is. (Wait. Don't make *that* bet!) A wise man once used the following analogy to try to express how difficult it was to accomplish a particular feat. He said, "it is easier for a camel to pass through the eye of a needle than it is for a rich man to give up his belongings and follow the straight and narrow path."

I have humbly changed a few words, but I think this message could be applied to gamblers: "It is easier for an elephant to do a tap dance on a fresh egg without cracking it than it is for a player to get ahead at a craps table and quit before giving back his winnings."

How you handle your bankroll ties in with money management and discipline, which supports the knowledge of the game you are about to learn. Don't discount bankroll as the springboard to your play. It may seem unimportant right now, but someday you will find out that this "white man does not speak with forked tongue." Before you get to the next chapter, go back over the last three sections. They are very important and will have a giant bearing on your ability to play sensibly.

3

Knowledge of the Game

Now we slide into the second chapter of the Big Four, which is nowhere close to being as important as money management and discipline, but since this is a basic, basic book, let's go over the object of the game.

When craps was played in the streets, long before the casinos arrived, the game was run by an individual or a group that we call bookies. They "booked" the game, which meant you were always playing against them. All that was needed was a set of dice containing six sides numbered from 1 to 6. Seven was the key number, as you can tell by examining one of these six-headed monsters. If the 1 is facing you, the 6 is on the opposite side. If 3 is staring you in the face, look at the opposite side and you'll see the 4. Finally, a 2 in front of you produces a 5 on the backside. They all total 7!

Take two dice in your hand, just as if you were playing craps, which requires you to throw two dice at a time across the table—but only throw one of them. No matter which number appears (1, 2, 3, 4, 5, or 6), you are halfway to a 7. That's how powerful that number is. When the bookie started his game, he would book all bets, and every player got the chance to throw the dice, going clockwise around the table. If you won, the bookie paid you. If you lost, he collected. The object of the game was very simple: The shooter would throw the dice on the first roll, which is called the come-out roll. He was "coming out" with his roll in an attempt to establish a point number, which would ignite that particular game.

With a set of dice, there are thirty-six combinations that could occur, using the totals of both dice. This we'll explain in depth later. For now, just understand the object of the game. Once you grasp that, everything else falls into place.

When you are the shooter, you are called a "right" bettor or a "do" bettor, and anyone who bets that you will make your point is also considered a right bettor or a do bettor. Those who bet against the shooter making his point are called "wrong" bettors or "don't" bettors. These are simply terms and have nothing to do with being right or wrong. Here are the basics of the game of craps:

1. Every player gets a chance to throw the dice. The one throwing the dice is the shooter. He or she places a bet on the pass line.
2. On the table's layout, there are six numbers shown: 4, 5, 6, 8, 9, and 10. These are called point numbers. (Look at the layout diagram. The pass line extends along the layout on both sides of the table.)
3. The shooter throws the dice.
   a. If a 7 or 11 is thrown, all right bettors (pass line bettors) win the amount of their bet.
   b. If a 2, 3, or 12 is thrown, all right bettors lose the amount of their bet.
4. If the shooter throws a 4, 5, 6, 8, 9, or 10, that is his or her point number and the dealer marks it with a puck. (We'll say the point is 6.)
5. The shooter continues to roll the dice until he or she makes that point (6 in this case), and all right bettors win. If a 7 is rolled, all right bettors lose.

6. When the shooter sevens-out, the dice are passed to the next shooter for a new game.

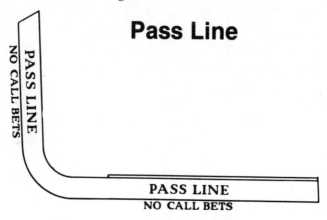

That is the game in a nutshell. I'll break it down even further:

1. The shooter puts a chip on the pass line.
2. Anybody around the table may also do the same, hoping the shooter will establish a point (4, 5, 6, 8, 9, or 10) and make that point again, before the 7 shows.
3. If the shooter throws 7 or 11 on his come-out roll, all players betting the pass line win.
4. If the shooter throws a 2, 3, or 12 on his come-out roll, all players betting the pass line lose.
6. If the shooter throws a 4, 5, 6, 8, 9, or 10 on the come-out roll, that is his point and he must throw that number again before throwing a 7.

Got it? We'll go over odds, side bets, and everything else as we go along, but this is the basic game. Simple, huh?

BANK CRAPS

Back on the streets, where craps originated, the bookie "faded," or "covered" all the action, unless there were so many bets that he would look for others to take part of the action. For example, when it was a person's turn to throw the dice, that player would lay out $500 (or any amount he wanted) on his roll. If the bookie didn't want all the action, he took what he wanted, say $300, and let the other players divide the rest. Then the bookie would announce what odds he would give on the other plays. He was in complete control.

When the casinos opened, they changed the game to what is called bank craps. In this game, it was possible to bet with or against the shooter, plus make a bevy of other bets. (We'll get into these bets shortly, some of which are place bets, come bets, and hard way bets.)

Both sides of the table are exactly the same (see the layout in next section), so the people on each side can make their bets with their dealer. Each dealer handles one side of the table. You can fit approximately eight players on each side of a craps table. The dealer with the stick is fittingly called the stick man. (The stick is used to retrieve the dice when they are rolled.) He runs the table, doing all the talking and explaining the point number, plus handling all proposition bets in the center of the table.

The dealers work in groups of four and rotate every twenty minutes: Three work the table and one takes a break. They each spend twenty minutes as the stick man, then twenty at one of the dealer posts, then twenty on a break.

The person sitting behind the table is called the box man or woman. He or she acts as a referee should discrepancies come up or decisions have to be made. If they cannot handle the situation, they call over the floor person that is assigned to that table. If the floor person cannot handle it, then the pit boss is called. There is one pit boss assigned to every section. A section might contain six craps tables, twelve blackjack tables and four roulette tables. The word of the pit boss is final.

Here is how a game begins:

1. The stick man has five dice in front of him, which he will pass

to the person who will be the next shooter.

2. The shooter must bet on either the pass line or on the don't pass line to be able to throw the dice. All the players around the table have the option of betting with the shooter by placing their own chips on the pass line, or against the shooter by betting on the don't pass line. (A quick glance at the layout will show you where the pass line and don't pass lines are.)

3. There is a pucklike device on the table that is black on one side and reads "Off" and white on the other and reads "On." When the shooter gets the dice to start his roll, the black side of the puck is face-up and the puck is off to the side of the table. It means the game has not yet started.

4. The shooter tosses the dice across the table, and they must both hit the far wall to be considered a valid throw. In our scenario, let's say the shooter throws a 4 and 5 for a 9.

5. The stick man announces: "Nine, nine, we're out on nine." That means everyone with a bet on the pass line wants that shooter to throw a 9 before a 7.

The game has begun, and the two dealers turn the white side of the puck face-up and place it on the 9 to indicate to everyone that this is the point.

As far as the bets on the pass and don't pass lines are concerned, the nine is their key. The shooter keeps throwing until he makes a 9 or until he sevens-out. There are many other bets that can be made, but this is the basic idea. We'll go over the odds very soon, so just make sure you have a grasp of the start of the game before we go on.

THE LAYOUT

Before we get into the multiple betting options and the odds information, take a look at the layout of a craps table:

As stated, the left and right sides are exactly the same, so forget

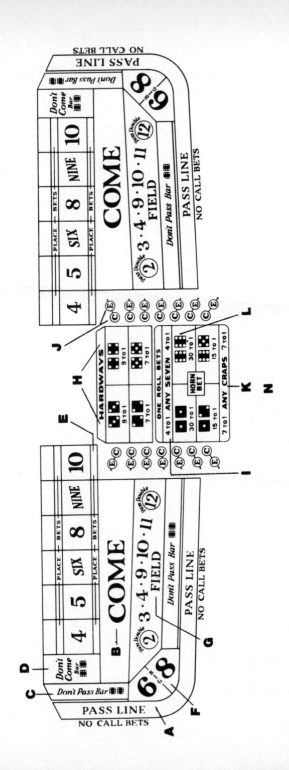

trying to memorize both sides. Let's follow according to the chart's lettering:

A. **Pass Line**   All "do" and "right" bettors place their chips here before the shooter establishes the point.

B. **Come**   After the shooter establishes the point, anyone can make a bet in the "come." The next roll pertains to that bet. It is exactly the same as the pass line in that while you are establishing a number for *that* roll, 7 or 11 wins; 2, 3, or 12 loses; and 4, 5, 6, 8, 9, or 10 gives you another point, called a come bet, just as the pass line bet is called a pass line point.

C. **Don't Pass**   All "don't" or "wrong" players make their bets here.

D. **Don't Come**   After the point is established, chips can be bet for the next roll of the dice to set additional don't numbers. Again, 7 or 11 loses; 12 is a tie, or a push; 2 or 3 wins for the don't bettor. 4, 5, 6, 8, 9, or 10 gives you another don't point.

E. **Place Bets**   Includes numbers 4, 5, 6, 8, 9, and 10. These numbers may be "placed," or taken down, anytime you wish. The dealers handle all these wagers, so merely drop your chips on the table and tell him which numbers you wish to place.

F. **Big 6 and Big 8**   Available in Las Vegas casinos and in some smaller casinos, but not in Atlantic City. Stupid bet. The house pays even money if you put your money on the big 6 or big 8. If you place the 6 or 8 with the dealer, you get paid $7 for your $6. Which would you rather get paid, $6 for $6 or $7 for $6? *Never* play the big 6 or big 8.

G. **Field**   A one-roll bet that can be made at any time.

H. **Hard Way Bet**   A proposition bet that the 4, 6, 8, or 10 can be made the "hard" way before either a seven or an "easy" number shows. (Example: hard 8: 4-4. Easy 8: 2-6, 6-2, 3-5, 5-3).

I. **Any Seven**   A one-roll bet that a 7 shows on the next roll.

J. **C or E**   A one-roll bet that either any craps (C) or an 11 (E) will show. The diagram shows where the chips are placed, in relation to where you're standing at the table.

K. **Any Craps**   A one-roll bet that a 2, 3, or 12 will show. Pays 7 to 1.

L. **Horn**   A combination one-roll bet on the three craps numbers plus the 11.

M. **Dealer**   His or her position at the table.

N. **Stick Man**   His or her position at the table.

O. **Box Person**   His or her position at the table.

It is not hard to learn the table, and subsequent chapters will go into each term in detail. So read on.

THE GAME

There will be later sections on the don't bettor, so right now we'll focus on do bettors or right bettors. You already know that playing simply means putting a bet on the pass line, the shooter establishing a point of either 4, 5, 6, 8, 9, or 10, and either making his point or sevening out. That's the basic idea.

Let's take that shooter and see what could happen as he attempts to establish a point with his come-out roll. The come-out roll is the first roll of a new game, when the shooter begins his game. Here is the complete list of thirty-six combinations that could occur:

Number That Shows	Combinations	Ways to Roll It
2	1-1	1
3	1-2, 2-1	2
4	1-3, 3-1, 2-2	3
5	1-4, 4-1, 2-3, 3-2	4
6	1-5, 5-1, 2-4, 4-2, 3-3	5
7	1-6, 6-1, 2-5, 5-2, 3-4, 4-3	6
8	2-6, 6-2, 3-5, 5-3, 4-4	5
9	3-6, 6-3, 4-5, 5-4	4
10	4-6, 6-4, 5-5	3
11	5-6, 6-5	2
12	6-6	1

The above chart shows you how many ways you can roll each number (2 through 12). Notice that dreaded 7 and the total number of ways it can be made. Here's what could happen with each of these numbers, depending on what the shooter throws on his come-out roll:

Seven: All pass line bettors win even money.
Eleven: All pass line bettors win even money.
Two: Craps. Pass line bettors lose.
Three: Craps. Pass line bettors lose.
Twelve: Craps. Pass line bettors lose.

On the come-out roll, which starts the game, the shooter and all bettors win even money if the shooter throws a 7 or 11. If the shooter rolls craps (2, 3, or 12), all pass line bettors on the pass line lose their bets. The other numbers (4, 5, 6, 8, 9, and 10) are the point numbers. Note: Pass line bettors will win even money on eight occasions, the total number of ways to roll the 7 or 11. They will lose on four occasions, the total number of ways to throw craps. Four, 5, 6, 8, 9 or 10 is the shooter's point. The dealer marks the number with the puck, and the shooter must roll that number before he or she rolls a 7.

This is crucial: there are six ways to roll a 7—more than any other number. So after the shooter establishes his point, his odds, or chances of winning, are always less than his chances of losing. Consider the odds when the shooter establishes his point. If it is:

- Four: There are three chances of winning, six chances of losing with the 7. Odds are 2 to 1 against the right bettor.
- Ten: There are three chances of winning and six chances of losing. Odds are 2 to 1 against the right bettor.
- Five: There are four ways of winning versus six ways of losing. Odds are 3 to 2 against the right bettor.
- Nine: There are four ways of winning versus six ways of losing. Odds are 3 to 2 against the right bettor.

- Six: There are five ways of winning and six ways of losing. Odds are 6 to 5 against right bettor.
- Eight: There are five ways of winning and six ways of losing. Odds are 6 to 5 against right bettors.

Obviously, the 6 and 8 are the best point numbers, because the odds are only 6 to 5 against you (the right bettor), and you have more ways of winning—five to be exact. Just remember that after the point is established, the odds swing against the right bettor. That's because after the point is established (4, 5, 6, 8, 9, or 10), the odds on the dreaded 7, which can be made six ways, are always more than any of the numbers that became the point.

Look at the charts showing the total number of ways to make each of the point or place numbers. They are always fewer than the six ways to make that 7!

ODDS

This is the most difficult section, because I have to get technical and show you how to figure out odds. I hate doing it, but you must learn odds, and it is really very simple to grasp. The key is remembering how many ways to make the 7: six ways! All odds are based on how many ways you can make your point versus the number of ways you can roll a 7.

Let's say you put a $5 chip on the pass line and the point is a 4. The odds against you winning are 2 to 1 because you have three ways of rolling a four (3-1, 1-3, 2-2) and six ways of getting hit with the seven (1-6, 6-1, 2-5, 5-2, 3-4, 4-3).

The casinos allow you to take free odds behind your pass line bet in either equal amounts or double, triple, and even ten times odds. Let's say you bet $5 on the pass line and 4 is your point. Even though you only have three ways of making that 4, versus six ways to lose with the 7, the house only pays you even money. So they allow you to take free odds behind that pass line bet. If you take single odds, which is another $5 bet, you'll get paid the true odds of making that point against the 7. In the case of the 4 or 10, each of which can be made three ways, a $5 odds bet would net you $10. A double odds bet of $10 would net you $20. A triple odds bet of $15 would net you $30.

Some casinos allow you to take ten times odds off your basic pass line bet, so if you bet $5 on the pass line, you can take ten times that $5 bet for an odds bet of $50. If the shooter rolls a 4 or 10, you would be paid $100.

The 5 or 9, which can be made four ways, would be a 3 to 2 payoff and net you $75 for your $50 odds. The 6 or 8 has odds of 6 to 5 against you, so a $50 odds bet would net you $60. Get it? Just remember: The true odds are based on the number of ways you can make your number versus the six ways of making that darn 7. Now you got it!

Let's continue our illustration. Your point is 4 and you are facing a 1 to 2 or 3 to 6 chance of winning. You should always take the odds when you bet the pass line, so as to increase the value of your pass line bet. If you do not take the odds, you'll only get even money for your pass line bet. Taking the odds, which are paid off in the exact ratio of ways to make the point against the 7, increases the value of your pass line wager. (All of these examples are based on $5 bets. If you bet higher, simply adjust the payoff.)

Point Odds	Odds Bet	True Odds	Payoff
4	$5	2–1	$10
5	$6	6–4, 3–2, 9–6	$9 for $6
6	$5	6–5	$6
8	$5	6–5	$6
9	$6	6–4, 3–2, 9–6	$9 for $6
10	$5	2–1	$10

Note: In the case of the 5 and 9, the odds are 6 to 4, 3 to 2, or 9 to 6 against you, so you can take odds in $6 increments and be paid $9 for every $6 bet, which comes out to a 3 to 2 payoff. The 4, 6, 8, and 10 points can take $5 odds bets.

Naturally, you're paid even money for your pass line bet of $5, and then the dealer will pay you odds based on the point number. Here are the payoffs for a $10 pass line bet with double odds:

Point Odds	Odds Bet	True Odds	Payoff
4	$10	2–1	$20
5	$10	3–2, 6–4, 9–6	$15
6	$10	6–5	$12
8	$10	6–5	$12
9	$10	3–2, 6–4, 9–6	$15
10	$10	2–1	$20

Since it is easy for the dealer to pay 3 to 2 on a $10 odds bet with the 5 and 9, you can take $10 odds and get 3 to 2 ($15), or you can take any even-amount odds bet for the 5 or 9, since they pay you 3 to 2. For example, $8 odds pays $12, $6 pays $9, $12 pays $18.

It isn't difficult to grasp. The odds increase the value of the pass line wager. If you bet $5 on the pass line and 10 is the point number, you are getting even money, or $5 for every $5 bet. By taking double odds of $10, you get (if the point is made) $5 for your pass line bet and $20 for your 2 to 1 payoff on the $10 odds, for a total of $25. Now, instead of $5 for $5 wagered, you're getting $8.33 for each $5 bet (on a total of $15 bet).

I hate explaining odds because people *think* it is complicated, yet all of my examples are to get them to realize that it is just simple logic. (There's that Little Three again.) Go over it one more time. Odds have a logical payoff formula: the total amount of ways to make the 7 versus the total number of ways to make the number in question.

VIGORISH

While we're on this subject, let me remind you that casinos allow double and triple odds to be taken, which reduces the house vigorish. The people who teach craps from a standpoint of vigorish would scream at me for not mentioning this term, so it is my duty to show you what it is. For the record, vigorish is simply the "edge" or "hammer" that the casinos have going for them. It is there, but don't worry about it.

Below is the house "vig," or casino's advantage, you are fighting with different craps bets (be wary of the highest numbers, which indicate greater advantages for the house):

Bet	Casino Pays	House Advantage
Pass line	Even money	1.41
Pass line and single odds	Even money and true odds	0.84
Pass line and double odds	Even money and true odds	0.60
Don't pass line (bar 12)	Even money	1.40
Don't pass line and single odds	Even money and true odds	0.83
Don't pass line and double odds	Even money and true odds	0.59
Come bet	Even money	1.41
Don't come (bar 12)	Even money	1.40
Pass line and triple odds	Even money and true odds	0.55
Don't pass line and triple odds	Even money and true odds	0.54
Place bet: 4 or 10	9–5	6.67
Place bet: 5 or 9	7–5	4.00
Place bet: 6 or 8	7–6	1.52
Buy: 4 or 10	2–1 (5% commission)	4.76
Lay bet: vs. 4 or 10	1–2 (5% commission)	3.03
Lay bet: vs. 5 or 9	2–3 (5% commission)	2.50
Lay bet: vs. 6 or 8	5–6 (5% commission)	1.82
Field (2–1 on 2 and 12)	Even money	5.56
Field (3–1 on 12 and 2–1 on 2)	Even money	3.70
Any seven	4–1	16.67
Any Craps	7–1	11.10
Eleven	15–1	11.10
Hard way 4 or 10	7–1	11.10
Hard way 6 or 8	9–1	9.09

I do not worry much about odds because the house always has an advantage, and putting too much emphasis on odds is a joke. My friend, Hope Less, is a hopeless case at the table and a big advocate of vigorish. He makes a bet on the pass line and brags that he has to take quadruple odds to reduce the house vig to 0.37 against him. After patting himself on the back with his free hand for making such a smart move, he slides his left foot into his mouth as he drops $30 on the table and announces to the dealer: "Hey Mac, gimme fifteen dollars on the four [6.67 percent vig], ten dollars on the hard six [9.09 vig], two dollars on any craps [11.10 vig], and three dollars on any seven [a staggering 16.67 vig]." What a fool!

Let me give you two more examples why I think vig is overrated. My friend, Jean Neeus, is a genius when it comes to numbers. She tells me she only plays blackjack because the house vig is only 1.51 against her. I ask her, "Are you good at basic strategy?" She looks puzzled and replies, "What is basic strategy?" For her information, basic strategy has to do with the moves you make in blackjack with your two cards versus the dealer's up-card. Without basic strategy, the vig against this "genius" is up in the triple digits.

I'll illustrate one more example—this time using sports. Suppose the Green Bay Packers are playing the Dallas Cowboys and you wanna win $100 betting on Dallas. Regardless of the line on the game and whether you bet the favorite or the underdog, you have to lay $110 to win $100. I bet sports *every day*, and so do all professional sports bettors. We are paying 10 percent vig. Did you hear that? 10 percent vig!

Vigorish is there every time we make a bet. It is the thing we are up against in life, just as we are up against pollution, bad drivers, crooked politicians, a weak economy, fatal illnesses, and mothers-in-law. Still, we live with it all, because it is part of the game of life. Vigorish is a part of gambling. Just don't worry about it.

PASS LINE/COME LINE

Let's review what we've gone over so far about craps. For now, forget about money management and all other betting principles. Let's say you're at a craps table and you buy in for $100.

1. The shooter picks up the dice for his come-out roll. You place $5 on the pass line. You are a right bettor.
2. The shooter throws an eleven and you win $5. You pick up the $5 in chips and again bet $5 on the pass line.
3. The shooter throws a crap 12, so you lose your $5 and replace the bet.
4. The shooter throws a 5, which becomes your point. You take $10 odds behind the point, as the dealer slides the puck white-side up over to the 5.
5. You now have a $5 pass line bet but want to get another number working. (We haven't covered place bets yet.) So you put $5 on the come.

The shooter bangs a 4, and the dealer slides your $5 chip into the 4 box and looks to you for odds. You drop $10 on the table and merely say, "Odds, please." This is the same thing as taking odds on your pass line bet. The only difference is that the dealer handles your chips. He places your odds bet on top of your come bet, letting it hang over the bottom chip to indicate odds.

Important note: When you make a come bet and the dealer moves your chips to that particular come number (in this case, the 4), he places the chips in such a way to indicate where you are standing at the table. This way, if he goes on a break, the next dealer knows whose bet it is by the positioning of the chips. If your come number hits, the dealer pays your flat bet plus odds and slides the payoff and the bet to the spot on the table that is indicated by the position in that box. Now, back to our example. You have a pass line bet of $5 on the 5 with $10 odds, and a $5 come bet on the 4 with $10 odds. As we already said, you want another number working, so you put $5 on the come. The shooter throws a craps 3 and you lose that come bet, just like you would have if it was on the pass line in a come-out situation.

You place another $5 chip in the come, and a 6 is rolled. The dealer moves the $5 bet to the 6 to coincide with where you are standing. You drop him $10 odds on your 6, which will pay you $12 if the 6 is thrown. (True odds on the 6 is $6 to $5.) You now have a $5 pass line bet on the 5, with $10 odds and two $5 come bets on the 4 and 6, both with double odds. You decide that is enough.

The shooter tosses a 4 and you pop out your chest because you have a come bet. The dealer puts $5 next to the base bet and $20 (2 to 1 payoff) for the $10 odds bet. He pushes your original $15 bet on the 4 with odds, plus $25 profit in front of you. Now you only have the pass line bet on the 5 and the come bet on the 6 working—both with double odds. You drop $5 in the come to establish another number.

The shooter throws a 7. You die a little. You lose the pass line bet of $5 with $10 odds and the come bet on the 6 with odds. However, that new $5 bet on the come is a come-out roll, and since the shooter threw a 7, you win $5. The dealer gives you your $5 bet plus $5 profit. Since the shooter sevened-out, the dice pass to the next shooter and a new game begins.

For that game, you lost $30 on the pass line bet with odds and the come bet on the 6 with odds but had a profit of $25 when the 4 hit, plus $5 on the last 7. You break even for that shooter. The stick man slides five dice to the next shooter, who selects two, and a new game will start.

Take a brief look back at this sequence and notice how easy it is to follow. My friend, Watt E. Cey, just woke up and asked me to repeat it. He missed a few things. Go back and check it out before you go on.

COME BETTING

Old-time craps players have been betting the pass line, taking odds and establishing two come numbers with odds, and hoping for Lady Luck to allow the shooter to throw for three days. It won't happen because of the power of that 7. Occasionally, you'll get a nice roll, but most of the time the lack of money management will destroy an otherwise smart craps player.

Why do all of these oldtimers play the same way? Because all of the books tell them that pass line with odds and come bets with odds are the way to play. I vehemently disagree with this nonsense. I will try to get you to use place betting as your way to go, but I still want you to understand the whole table. Upcoming sections on place betting will show you my way.

The reason all of the books stress come betting is to urge the players to take advantage of the vigorish. Baloney! Let's say a craps player puts $5 on the pass line. A 4 shows, and he takes $10 odds. His vig is down to 0.6 percent with that double odds bet. The dealer smiles at him for being so smart. The house edge is reduced to 0.6 because our hero is getting the true 2 to 1 payoff for his odds bet. Let's say I am at that same table and have no bet on the pass line or come line.

Naturally, I would never bet the 4 or 10 since there are only three ways to make each of those numbers. I *never* touch them, but for the sake of this example, I will. I drop $15 on the table and tell the dealer to place the 4. She looks down her nose at me because, even though I have the same amount of money at risk ($15), I am fighting a house advantage of 6.67 percent—more than ten times higher than the genius next to me.

Anyway, the shooter bangs out a 4, and the dealer pays this guy $5 for his pass line bet and $20 for his $10 odds bet. He has $25. The dealer scornfully pays me $27 ($9 to $5) for my place bet on the 4. I get $27. My fellow player is fighting a vig of 0.6 percent and wins $25. I am fighting a vig of 6.67 percent, and win $27—$2 more than he won. Ain't that odd! Don't bother trying to figure it out—the reason is you only get even money for your pass line bet. No amount of odds can offset the house's edge once that point is established.

No matter how much odds he takes—even one hundred times odds—I'll still get more because of the drain on the player with that even payoff on the original pass or come line bet. Naturally, the pass line bettor has the added edge of eight ways to make the 7 or 11 on the come out, but he could also lose four ways with craps, giving him only a +4 edge that the payoffs do not make up.

One more example: if you leaf back to an earlier chapter, you'll see the number of ways each number can be made:

- 4 and 10 can be made three ways each.
- 5 and 9 can be made four ways each.
- 6 and 8 can be made five ways each.

Experienced craps players always hope for the 6 or 8 to become the point because obviously there are more ways to make these numbers, so there are more ways to win—and they are 100 percent right.

Okay, let's say Jean E. Yuss also hopes for the 6 or the 8 as she places her bet on the pass line. She has ten ways of getting the 6 or the 8—but she has fourteen ways of getting the 4, 5, 9, or 10. The odds are 14 to 10 against her getting the 6 or 8. Why not just bypass the come-out roll and place the 6 and 8? You'd have them 100 percent of the time. Why not indeed? This will be explored in detail very soon.

I do not bet the pass line or come line because I want the 6 and 8 all the time, not a 14 to 10 edge against me. Here is what I do:

1. Bypass the come-out roll.
2. After the point is established, I drop my chips on the table and ask the dealer to place the 6 and 8.

Now I have the 6 and 8 100 percent of the time. Pass line bettors and come bettors may have the vig on their side, but that's a water pistol in comparison to having the choice of pointing a gun at the table and getting the two most powerful "right" numbers working for you *all* the time. That means ALL of the time—absorb that!

Don't play the come!

REVIEW: BASIC TERMS

Before we go much further in explaining this game, let's take a second to review some parts of the table and even acquaint you with a couple that will be forthcoming. You may like to refer back to the chapter with the craps layout to help with this update.

Buy-in The amount of money you buy in with at a table.

Come The bet the player makes to establish additional working numbers. The rules are exactly the same as those for the pass line. Win on 7 or 11, lose on 2, 3, or 12 for the chips that are working on that roll on the come line.

Come-Out Roll The first roll of the dice by the shooter to set the point.

Craps This is when the shooter throws a 2, 3, or 12 on the come-out roll and all pass line bettors lose, or, players betting in the come and the next roll is craps. The come bettors lose their bet.

Don't Come Line This is when the player attempts to establish additional "don't" numbers. (We'll explore "don't" betting in depth.)

Don't Pass Line This is for the player betting that the shooter does not make his established point.

Dork A stupid player.

Field A one-roll bet that the shooter will throw a 2, 3, 4, 9, 10, 11, or 12 on the next roll. The bet is lost if 5, 6, 7, or 8 is thrown.

Hard Ways There are five ways to make an 8. If it is thrown as 2-6, 6-2, 3-5, 5-3, it is considered an easy 8. If it is thrown 4-4, it is considered a hard 8. The same is true with a hard 4, 6, or 10. An "Easy" number or a 7 will beat a hard way bet. Let's say you toss a $1 chip into the center of the table and say, "Hard six, please!" Your bet stays there until a decision is reached or you ask to take the bet back. You win with 3-3. You lose on any 7 or any other combination of 6 (2-4 or 5-1).

Hedge   Betting both "right" and "wrong," cutting losses way down. For example, a don't bettor has a don't bet with the 10 showing. Then he or she goes back and plays a hard 10 or places the 10 to reduce possible losses. Excellent bet.

House Advantage   The "edge," or "vigorish," that the casino holds over every bet. The percentages may differ, but the casino *always* has some type of advantage in their favor.

Laying Odds   The "wrong" bettor "lays" odds against his don't pass or don't come bet. (To be discussed in chapters on "don't" betting.)

Natural   A 7 or 11 that is thrown on the first (come-out) roll. All "right" bettors win their pass line bets. A natural 7 or 11 that is thrown on the come-out roll will beat any person betting on the don't pass.

Odds   The extra bet players make either when betting "right" or "wrong," in addition to a pass or don't pass bet. Odds allow you to back up your basic bet.

Pass Line   This is where all "right" bettors make their bet on the come-out roll.

Place Bets   The opportunity to place the numbers 4, 5, 6, 8, 9, or 10 anytime you want. You can also take off place bets anytime you want. Excellent bet. (Further chapters will be devoted to this method of play.)

Point   The numbers 4, 5, 6, 8, 9, or 10 that the shooter establishes and must throw again to win the game (before the 7 shows).

Press   When you win a bet and increase, you "press," your wager. It is called pressing your bet.

Proposition Bets   Anytime you make bets on the hard ways, the

11, any 7, or craps. (These bets are made in the center of the table when you toss your chips to the stick man.) Any of these bets are called proposition, or "prop" bets.

Right Bettor   Term for players betting on the shooter to make his point and place numbers. Also called do bettors.

Seven-Out   When shooters establish a point and lose when the 7 shows; they "seven out"—not crap out.

Taking Odds   The "right" bettor "takes odds" behind his pass line bet or his come bet.

Wrong Bettor   Term for players who bet that the shooter does not make his numbers. Also called "don't" bettors.

Yo   Slang word for 11.

Some of these terms were already mentioned, and some we'll go into in a bit later. Are you catching the drift? If not, go back and review the parts that are not clear.

PLACE BETTING

A couple of sections back, I went over the come line, which I hate doing and for good reason. In this section, I will explain place betting and then compare these two theories of betting. I'll let you decide which you think is better.

Read and grasp this part, because if you are just starting out at craps, this could very well be the way to go about it. A few pages back, I told you that over 90 percent of all right bettors play the pass line and take odds because that was the way they were taught, and it was handed down through the years. Yet these same players yearn for 6 or 8 to be their point numbers because they can be made the most numbers of ways (five each). I know I told you all of this before, but for the benefit of my friend, Rhea Repeat, who forgot, I'll tell you again—because it is so important.

Anyway, these fanatics of pass line play were so obsessed with the 6 and 8 that if their point was 4, 5, 9, or 10, they immediately placed the 6 and 8. You see, the casinos allow you to make bets on any of those six place numbers anytime you like, without having to establish them with pass line or come betting. This means that if your pass line number becomes a 10, you could drop $12 on the table and tell the dealer: "Place the six and eight please." That shooter would have a point number of 10 with odds and also pick up the 6 and 8, which he wanted in the first place. My contention is, why go worrying about betting the pass line if you're afraid of the 4, 5, 9, or 10 becoming your point?

This is what you could do:

1. Bypass the come-out roll by not betting on the pass line.
2. After the point is established, either 4, 5, 6, 8, 9, or 10, place the 6 and 8.

This way, you get the two numbers you wanted every game—100 percent of the time. What is so hard about that? Place betting is an art that should be perfected. You can place the 4, 5, 9, or 10 in any increments of $5 bets. You can place the 6 or 8 in increments of $6 bets. The payoffs are shown below, along with the house advantage and true odds.

Number	True Odds	House Pays	House Advantage
4	2–1	$9–$5	6.67%
5	3–2 or 6–4	$7–$5	4.00%
6	6–5	$7–$6	1.51%
8	6–5	$7–$6	1.51%
9	3–2 or 6–4	$7–$5	4.00%
10	2–1	$9–$5	6.67%

This table is easy to understand. If you place the 4 or 10 for $5, you should be paid $10 because there are three ways against making the 4 or 10, as opposed to six ways of making the 7. The house, however, pays $9 to $5, a high 6.67 edge (holding $1 per bet back) instead of $10 to $5. If you place the 5 or 9 for $5, you should be paid $7.50, which is the true odds of 3 to 2, or 6 to 4, or 9 to 6, or 7 ½ to 5. The casino pays you $7 instead of $7.50 for every $5 bet, which means they beat you out of 50¢ on every $5 winning bet.

If you place the 6 or 8 for $6, the house pays you $7 for your $6 wager. You should be paid $6 to $5, which is the correct odds of being able to make the 6 or 8 as opposed to the six ways of making the 7. The house holds only 20¢ for every winning wager, a minuscule 1.51 advantage.

Obviously, the 6 and 8 are great moves, the 5 and 9 are not too bad, and the 4 and 10 are a joke. I *never* bet the 4 or 10—never, never, ever, ever. Why should I give up $1 for every $5 winning wager? I shouldn't, so I won't place the 4 or 10. This is not the last chapter on place betting—only the first. Do not go on until you fully understand this aspect of place betting.

THE POWER OF PLACE BETTING

I have written ten books on gambling, the titles of which are listed in the back of this one. There is a basic book on craps, which is the next step up from this one, and then comes *Advanced Craps*—the best book ever written on gambling (the opinions of others). In it, I have over one hundred chapters on money management and discipline. Read it. In the chapter "Knowledge of the Game," I wrote a section on place betting that lists all of the significant facts about this excellent method of playing craps. I'm repeating some of that chapter here because it covers what I'm trying to get across.

- Place bets are the six numbers spread across the layout (4, 5, 6, 8, 9, 10).
- Bets can be made, taken down, increased, or decreased whenever you wish.
- Place bets are automatically off on the come-out roll, which means if a player establishes a point (we'll say a 9), and you placed

the 5, 6, and 8, and the shooter makes that 9, he would then need to start a new game by establishing a new point number. If you had any place numbers still up on the board, they would be automatically off on the new come-out roll. You would not win if the shooter threw one of those place numbers, trying to establish a point, and you would not lose if the shooter threw a 7 on that subsequent come-out roll. Place bets are off on any come-out roll, unless you tell the dealer they are "working" (in action).

- You can have action on the come-out roll by merely informing the dealer that your place bets are "working" (in action).
- At any time during a roll you can tell the dealer that your place bets are "off." The dealer will place an "off" button on your outside bet to signify that you have no action on any place bets.
- You can get back in action after one roll, or as many as you like, by merely stating, "Back in action."
- Place bets stay until you ask for them to be taken down or until the 7 does it for you.
- Place bets do not pay true odds, but the house vig on 6 or 8 is only 1.51 percent, one of the best bets in the house.
- Vig on 5 or 9 is 4 percent.
- Vig on 4 or 10 is 6.67 percent.
- Increments in place betting are based on these payoffs:
  6 and 8, $7 to $6.
  5 and 9, $7 to $5.
  4 and 10, $9 to $5.
- Based on the payoffs listed above, the house makes the following dollar amount on each wager:
  6 and 8: 20¢ on each $5 bet.
  5 and 9: 50¢ on each $5 bet.
  4 and 10: $1 on each $5 bet.
- For instance, if you place the 4 for $5, the true odds are 2 to 1, so you should be paid $10 for the winning bet. The house pays you $9. That's a buck you lose on that swing.

Do you think you have an idea of what place betting is? In a subsequent chapter, we'll compare the place betting methods with come betting methods. You can make up your own mind as to which is better.

EXAMINING COME BETS

Let's look at some of the good reasons for betting the come line, then we'll examine the negative side.

Good points of the come bet:

- The vig you're fighting against is only 1.41, no matter what the point is.
- With single odds, the vig is reduced to 0.8 percent.
- By taking triple odds, you reduce the house vig to 0.6 percent.
- With your initial bet on the pass or come line, a 7 or 11 will give you an instant even-money payoff.

In my opinion, too much emphasis is placed on the word vigorish, especially after the example I gave you where placing a $15 bet on the 4 gave you more of a return than a $5 pass line bet with double odds. The dollar amount on both bets is $15, while the vig against the pass line bettor is only 0.6 percent, as opposed to a vig of 6.67 percent for the place bettor. Yet the place bettor won more money for his winning bet. Vigorish is overrated.

The bottom line is not vigorish but cutting your chances of losing. Place bets can be taken down any time. Pass line and come wagers are contract bets and must stay until a decision is reached. Let's look at the negative side of come bets. Pay close attention.

- You have to make the come number *twice:* once to establish it and once to win. You can make a wager on the place bets, take a hit, and come right off.
- You have to take the number that "comes," even though it may be the difficult 5 or 9, or the extremely tough 4 or 10.

- You have four rolls on the come bet that give you instant losses (2, 3, or 12), which cut into the eight-plus rolls of 7 or 11. In other words, a bet in the come will win instantly on 7 or 11 and lose instantly on 2, 3, or 12. You must, however, take the come number that shows.
- Come bets come down after a hit, and to get back up you need to reestablish them. Let's say you bet the come and I place the 6 and 8:

  1. The 6 shows and your come is established, while I collect a payoff.
  2. The 6 hits and we both collect.
  3. The 6 scores again and you reestablish your come. I get paid.
  4. The 6 bangs out again. We both collect. That was four 6s: you collected twice, I collected four times. Enough said.

Look at the second point above. You can hope and pray all you want for the 6 or 8 to come. There are solid odds that you have ten chances for the 6 or 8 and fourteen for the 4, 5, 9, or 10.

The place bettor can choose his number; the come bettor cannot. I have saved this example for last. Be sure you understand it. It starts with this rule: come bets work on the come-out roll, while odds don't! This means that once you establish a come bet or two or three of them, you should take odds to diminish the worthless value of a bet that pays even money while the house holds a large edge with the six ways for the 7 to be made.

During the course of a game, you have a $5 bet on the pass line with odds, covering the point of 6, for example. You then establish two other come numbers, 5 and 10, both with odds. You're feeling pretty good, especially when the shooter hits 6, your point number. You almost stretch a tendon in your elbow patting yourself on the back while you slide another chip on the pass line to establish a new point. Your 5 and 10 come bets with odds are still sitting there. You smile broadly as the shooter throws a 7 on his come-out roll to start another game, and the dealer matches your pass line bet—but then you die as he takes down your come bet on the 5 and your come bet on the 10, because come bets work on the come-out roll and 7 beats you.

You get your odds back because odds don't work on the come-out roll, so even if the shooter banged out a 10 as his new point, you'd still only get the amount of your base bet and your odds back. Those come bets have no protection on a come-out roll.

A couple of additional things: since there are four ways to make a 5 and three ways to make a 10, you only had a total of seven ways to win one of those come bets. The six ways to make a 7, which takes down both come bets, is almost as many as the total you had for two separate bets. You can lose both bets with a 7, but need separate hits to collect both.

Go back and read this last example again—and again and again.

Finally: Place bets do not work on the come-out unless you tell the dealer, "Working." Personally, I leave them off, but you have the option. When you score on a place bet, you can increase, decrease, or take the bet down altogether. With a hit on the come, the house pays you and gives you your bet back with odds. Now you have to start all over to reestablish those come bets. There are no options to practicing money management.

This was a long chapter but an enlightening one! Did you zero in on all the minuses? The next chapter goes over the pros and cons of place betting, in case you're still hanging out in undecided land.

EXAMINING PLACE BETS

Let's do the same thing here as we did with the come bets. Let's weigh the pros and cons of place bets:

Cons:

1. There is a higher vigorish against you (if you're worried about vig), especially with the placing of the 4, 5, 9, or 10.

That's it! That's the only disadvantage I can see. You're fighting a vigorish of 4.00 percent when placing the 5 or 9 and fighting 6.67 percent when placing the 4 or 10. I never place the 4 or 10, or have I said that before?

Pros:

1. You have a choice of which numbers you want to place.
2. Place numbers are automatically off on the come-out roll, unless you stipulate that they are working.
3. You can take down your place bets any time you wish.
4. You can adjust place bets up or down any time you like.

The first point here is all-important for the player who wants to bet only the 6 or 8. They can get the 6 and 8 100 percent of the time.

The second point here allows you the choice of whether or not you want come-out rolls to beat you. In fact, anytime during the course of a game, while you have place bets in action, you can tell the dealer, "Off." He will put an off button on top of your chips and you have no action until you tell him, "Working."

The third point on the list gives you the option of taking all or part of your place bets off any time you want. This is especially beneficial for players who like to take one or two hits and come down.

The fourth point is the main one because it gives you the power to adjust your bets up, down, or off, at your discretion.

That's about it! Make your choice—you know where I stand.

BUYING THE NUMBER

Here we go again, explaining a move that is designed to cut the house vig from 6.67 to 5 percent. That's like saying a fall from a fifth-story window is better than a tumble out of a seventh-story one. My humble opinion is that both falls hurt.

Anyway, when you place the 4 or 10 and they pay you $9 for every $5 wagered, you are getting beat a buck. They should pay $10 (a 2 to

1 payoff). That gives the house a 6.67 percent vigorish. So the casino throws you a bone. You still only get paid 9 to 5 for any bets of $5, $10, $15, or $20. When you reach a bet of $25 (a little too steep for the smaller-heeled $5 bettor), they let you "buy" the number instead of place it. This is only in effect for the 4 and 10, where the vigorish can be reduced from 6.67 to 5 percent. It's obvious that since the vig on placing the 5 or 9 is 4 percent, and on the 6 or 8 it is only 1.51 percent, the 5 percent shot is too high. So you still place the 5, 6, 8, and 9 when you reach $25 or higher per bet.

Let's say you wanna wager $25 on the 4 or 10. You drop $25 on the table and say, "Buy the four [or ten], please." The dealer puts your $25 bet in the box for your number and sets it up to coincide with where you are standing at the table. He then puts a "buy" button on that chip to indicate you bought that bet for a charge of 5 percent. He'll ask you for a dollar. It should be $1.25, but they eat the quarter. The extra dollar indicates you are buying the number, and you get 2 to 1 instead of 9 to 5 if your bet hits.

If the 4 shows, they pay you true odds of $50 for your $25 bet (2 to 1) instead of the $45 (9 to 5) that they give the $5 to $20 bettors. Naturally, if you bet $100 on the buy, your charge would be 5 percent, or $5. If it hits, you get $100 instead of $90, minus the 5 percent charge you paid.

Should you buy the 4 or 10? Yes, if you bet that high, because obviously it will pay more, but as I said before, I don't play the 4 or 10.

PROPOSITION BETS

Check back over the layout of the table, and right smack in the middle you'll see a whole bunch of odd-looking wagers, which entice a lot of players. For instance, the hard way bets, where you have to hit a double-digit total of the even numbers of 4, 6, 8, and 10, which compute to 4-4 being hard 8 versus 2-6, 6-2, 5-3, or 3-5 being an easy 8. Matching numbers are called hard ways. The other combinations of the even numbers of 4, 6, 8, and 10 are called easy.

Proposition bets

If you wish to wager that the shooter will throw a hard 8, you toss $1 toward the stick man and say, "Hard 8, please." If 4-4 shows before an easy 8 or a 7, you get paid 9 to 1. A $5 bet returns $45, so the temptation for a nice payoff is present.

Look, though, at how many ways you can lose: 3-5, 5-3, 2-6, 6-2, 1-6, 6-1, 2-5, 5-2, 3-4, or 4-3. That's ten ways of losing versus one way of winning. The odds are 10 to 1, and you should get paid 10 to 1. You don't, though. You get 9 to 1. The same is true for the hard 6. With the hard 4, there is one way of winning and eight ways of losing: 1-3, 3-1, and six ways to make 7. The hard 4 pays 7 to 1 when it should pay 8 to 1. I use the hard way bets to cut my losses on don't betting, which we'll look at later. The hard way bets are not great bets, but they're not bad either. I play them when a streak of them is showing. You'll see how in the next section.

There is also "any craps," a one-roll bet that pays 7 to 1 if the 2, 3, or 12 shows. Again, I only suggest you use this move to protect a high bet on the pass line, say $25. Then you can protect against a craps beating you by playing $3 any craps. I'd protect a $15 pass line bet with a $2 any craps, but not protect a lower wager.

Any craps is not a good bet, and even though it can be wagered at any time during the course of a game, I personally don't endorse it. You can actually bet any of these craps plays individually, such as:

"Gimme the two please." It pays 30 to 1. (It should pay 35 to 1 because there is one way to win and thirty-five ways to lose.) Bad bet.

"Gimme the twelve please." It pays 30 to 1. (It should pay 35 to 1 because there is one way to win and thirty-five ways to lose.) Also a bad bet.

"Gimme the ace-deuce craps please." It pays 15 to 1. (It should pay 17 to 1 because there are two ways to win and thirty-four ways to lose.) Another bad bet.

Then there is the *worst* bet on the table: a one-roll bet on *any* 7. It pays 4 to 1, but should pay 5 to 1. This bet is suicide, yet dorks at the table use it. *Please* don't play it!

The 11 is a one-roll bet that pays 15 to 1. It should pay 17 to 1 because there are two ways to win and thirty-four ways to lose. I use it to hedge and cut losses when I play the don't pass and/or the don't come. It is not otherwise suggested.

Don't bother rereading this chapter because I'm going to go over the proposition bets again in the next two sections. Here is a summary:

Hard ways: I play them when they are showing at a table and to hedge against don't bets on the 4, 6, 8, or 10.

Eleven (yo): Don't play on a whim. I use it only to protect a don't pass or don't come bet of $15 or higher. This hedge cuts possible losses.

Any craps: Don't play this sucker one-roll bet unless you use it to protect a pass line bet of $15 or higher. It definitely protects your bet on the pass line. Don't play it on a hunch.

Any seven: *Never* play it. That's a never as in NEVER. Period!

Let's move on.

THE THEORY OF "DON'T" BETTING

When we get to the chapter "Money Management," we'll go over how to bet and how to control your money. In this section, we go over what "don't" betting is all about. By now, you should know that to bet the "don't" side and lay odds requires a little bit more money, because you have to lay the true odds of making that number rather than the 7. Of course, you don't have to lay odds, but for those of you who do, it can become expensive.

Suppose you're betting $5 on the don't pass and 4 is your point. To lay odds to win another $5, you have to lay $10 to win $5 more. If you go for triple odds, you have to lay $30 to win $15. Along with your original don't bet of $5, that means you are betting $35 against that number to win $20. Even though the 7 gives you the edge, there will be many times that the shooter gets on a hot roll and bangs out numbers that will whack the don't bettor.

If you have three don't numbers working, with odds, you could fall way behind. The tough part is getting past that 7 or 11 on the come-out roll (which we will discuss), but once you do, the chances of your winning have increased drastically.

It is not my job or purpose to tell you how to bet, but depending on the side you choose ("right" or "wrong"), my intent is to help you cut losses and accept consistent returns. If you are betting "don't" and the table gets hot—leave that table if you lose three shooters in a row.

Just to wrap up the don't betting on the don't pass line, let's briefly review some items:

- Put your chip or chips on the don't pass line for the come-out roll.
- You're fighting the 7 or 11, which could show eight out of thirty-six rolls (22 percent of the time).
- You win with craps (1-1, 1-2, 2-1); you tie with a 12.
- When the point is established, the chances of winning swing to your favor.
- 4 or 10 is 6 to 3 in your favor.
- 5 or 9 is 6 to 4 in your favor.
- 6 or 8 is 6 to 5 in your favor.
- Laying odds against the 4 or 10 is 2 to 1 ($10 for $5, $20 for $10, $50 for $25, etc.).
- Laying odds against the 5 or 9 is 6 to 4 or 3 to 2 ($9 for $6, $15 for $10, $30 for $20, etc.).
- Laying odds against the 6 or 8 is 6 to 5 ($6 for $5, $12 for $10, $24 for $20, etc.).
- To protect a $15 bet on the don't pass line, you could bet $1 on the 11 (15 to 1), and you'd break even if the 11 shows.

After the don't pass number is established, you can sit on that bet, lay odds, hedge against it, or try to establish another number by going through the don't come (covered in the next section). That is the basic approach to "wrong" betting. Now we'll go a step further.

DON'T COME

This will be easy to grasp because the exact same rules that apply to the don't pass line will be applicable to the don't come box. Look at your craps table layout and you'll see the don't come bet sitting right next to the 4 or 10, depending on which side of the table you are on. Notice the letters are black, just like those on the don't pass line, to make them hard to see. The casinos prefer that the players concentrate on do betting.

Yet the casinos put the "Come" and "Any Seven" in bright red letters in order to draw your attention to them. For those of you who drive (but rarely pay attention to the traffic lights), red means stop. Keep that in mind when you play the red-lettered bets in craps.

Anyway, the don't come bet allows you to make additional wagers to get additional don't numbers working for you. To get these additional numbers, you go through the don't come box, and the next roll of the dice activates that bet, just like when you bet on the don't pass line. You cannot, however, make a don't come bet until *after* the point is established. This bet is similar to that of the "right" bettor who, after the initial point is established, uses the come to get additional do numbers.

But while the "right" bettor has the option to also place additional bets, the "wrong" bettor can only get additional numbers if he comes through the don't come box or lays higher amounts against different numbers. Read that again: "lays higher amounts against different numbers." This will be explained in a section appropriately titled, "Laying Against the Number."

For now, we are concentrating on picking up additional don't numbers for small bets by using the don't come box. Here's an example:

1. You put $5 on the don't pass and the shooter establishes a point of 9.
2. You want additional don't numbers, so you put $5 in the don't come box.
3. The next number will affect that bet either negatively or positively.

4. The don't come box is exactly the same as the don't pass line (win on 2 or 3, lose on 7 or 11, tie on 12.)

5. The shooter throws a 12. It is a push (tie) and there is no action.

6. The shooter throws a 2 or 3, and you win $5 and leave the bet there after you take your $5 profit.

7. The shooter throws an 11. You lose your don't come bet.

8. You replace your $5 don't come bet.

9. The shooter throws a 7. You lose your don't come bet but win your don't pass bet, because a 7 came up before the point of 9.

10. Another game starts, and you put $5 on the don't pass line.

11. The shooter sets 5 as his point and you put $5 in the don't come box.

12. The shooter throws a 6. The dealer takes your $5 wager and puts it behind the 6 in a position that indicates where you are standing at the table.

13. You now have a $5 no-5 on the don't pass line and a $5 no-6 from the don't come bet.

14. You want another don't come so you put $5 in the don't come box.

15. You win if 2 or 3 comes and push (tie) on 12. If 8 is rolled, your $5 don't come bet is moved behind the 8, and you now have no-5, no-6, and no-8 for $5 each.

16. Let's say the shooter sevens-out on the next roll. You win all three of your don't bets.

17. Let's say he did not seven-out, but made his point of 5. You lose your $5 on the don't pass line, but your no-6 and no-8 are still alive from the don't come box.

18. The don't come numbers "work" on the come-out roll, unless you say, "Off," to the dealer. Keep them working! Let's say the shooter starts a new game and throws a 7. If you had a chip on the don't pass line, you would lose that bet but win all don't

come bets. If he threw a 6 as his new point, you'd lose your
don't come 6 but now have no-6 as the don't pass number.

19. Go back to where the shooter made his point 5 and put $5 on
the don't pass line to start a new game.

20. If the shooter throws a 2 or 3, you win $5. If the shooter
throws an 11, you lose $5.

21. If the shooter throws a 7, you lose the don't pass line bet but
win $5 on each of your don't come numbers of 6 and 8, which
were established in the previous game.

22. Let's say he did *not* throw a 7 on that new come-out roll, but
established a new point of 4.

23. You now have a don't pass line bet of no-4 and your two don't
come bets of $5 each on the no-6 and no-8.

24. The shooter throws a 10: No action.

25. The shooter throws a 2, 3, 11, or 12: No action.

26. The shooter throws a 7: You win all three don't bets.

27. The new shooter comes out, and you start all over.

Got it? It is so obvious, logical, and easy to grasp. I hope you
breezed right along with me. My friend, Lee Tillslo, is a little slow in
grasping it. He has to go back and reread it, just like Rhea Repeet,
who needs it explained again and again. No problem! Just go back
over this example.

DON'T BETTING

This is gonna be really easy for you to understand, because it is
exactly the opposite of the do or right bettor. The don't side, or the
wrong bettor bets that the shooter does not make his point. Most
players bet "do" because they look for the big payoff, the possibility
of tripling their money.

The don't bettors have to grind out returns, hoping that they end
up at an ice cold table, where that 7 keeps popping up after the
shooter establishes his point. Neither right nor wrong bettors have a

big edge over the other, but the trick is being at a table going the way you decided to play, whether it be do or don't. In other words, if you are betting "right," you want a hot table. If you are betting "wrong," you want a cold table. It's called trends.

Since this section is devoted to teaching you about the game of craps, you'll have to wait until we get to the chapter "Money Management," to see *how* to bet. If you decide to be a don't bettor, you need to understand you will be in the minority at a table and be forced to endure the dirty looks and side remarks of the do bettors who think you're the enemy because you're betting against them. Don't let it bother you. They have the same choices you do.

Here are the differences between do and don't bettors:

- Do bettors put their bet on the pass line.
- Don't bettors put their bet on the don't pass line.
- The layout reads Don't Pass—Bar 12. It means the 12 is barred on the come-out roll and the don't bettors don't lose if 12 is thrown, it is a tie, or push.
- Do bettors win when the first roll (come-out roll) is 7 or 11.
- Don't bettors lose when the first roll (come-out roll) is 7 or 11.
- Do bettors lose if 2, 3, or 12 (craps) is thrown on the first roll.
- Don't bettors win when the first roll is 2 or 3. The 12 is a push.
- Do bettors like the 6 or 8 to become the point because they can be made the most ways.
- Don't bettors don't like 6 or 8 to become the point because they can be made the most ways.
- After the point is established, do bettors fear the 7 because it wipes them out.
- After the point is established, don't bettors want the 7 because it makes them a winner.
- After the point is established, do bettors can "take" odds on their number.

- After the point is established, don't bettors can "lay" odds against their number. (See the upcoming section.)
- On the come-out roll, do bettors have a tiny edge of 8 to 4 with 7 and 11 versus craps.
- After the point is established, don't bettors have a giant edge, as the 7 can be made more ways than any other point number (4, 5, 6, 8, 9, or 10).

There you have the simple comparisons between do and don't bettors. The next section is another one that explains odds—my least favorite topic.

LEARN THE ODDS

I have already indicated how much I hate this topic, but it's gotta be covered. On the other hand, the explanation is so logically simple that I hate to waste time on it, but then my friend, Watt E. Cey, will look at it and ask, "What did he say?" Let's see if I can break odds down so that it can be easily grasped:

1. A pass line bet only pays even money, so as soon as a point is set, the pass line player is in the hole against the six ways to make the 7.
2. The casino allows you to take odds behind your pass line bet and you will be paid according to your chances of making that point against the seven. For example, the point is 10. You have three ways of making that 10 (6-4, 4-6, 5-5). That gives the house a 6 to 3 or 2 to 1 edge because the 7 can be made six ways.
3. By taking $5 odds behind your $5 pass line bet, you now receive $15 for your $10 bet if the 10 is made. This improves the pass line bet value from $5 to $7.50.
4. With the 5 or 9, you take single odds of $6 to win $9 because the odds are 3 to 2, or 9 to 6, in favor of the house.

5. The 6 or 8 allows a $5 odds bet to be paid $6 to $5 because the odds are 6 to 5 in favor of the 7 versus the 6 or 8. Of course, you could take double or triple odds, but the arithmetic is the same.
6. If you bet the pass line, you should always take odds.
7. A don't bettor has the same choice as far as odds are concerned, except he is *laying* the odds, instead of taking them. He lays odds against his number because the 7 is now in his favor. Let's say 10 was the point and a don't bettor has $5 on the don't pass line and wants to get an additional bet on that point of 10. He has to lay the true odds of that 10 coming, which is 2 to 1 or 6 to 3 in his favor. There are six ways to make a 7 and three ways to make a 10, hence he lays 2 to 1, or $10 to win another $5.
8. If the point was 5 or 9, he would lay $9 to win $6 because the odds are 3 to 2, 6 to 4, or 9 to 6 for the ways to make the 7 over the 5 or 9. With the 6 or 8 as the point, don't bettors would lay $6 to win $5 because the true odds of the 7 versus the 6 or 8 is 6 to 5.
9. In other words, right bettors *take* true odds, and wrong bettors *lay* true odds.

This explains the total concept of taking or laying odds. I hope you understand now. Off in the corner, my three friends, I. M. Madork, Ed N. Sand, and Watt E. Cey are asking each other, "What's the pass line?" And you wonder why the casinos make so much money from dingdongs like this!

SHOULD YOU LAY ODDS?

Glad you asked. That is a great question, and any answer will move me further away from the hearts of the geniuses who insist that you should always take or lay odds. On the first theory, they are absolutely right. You should always take odds when you bet the pass line because that even-money payoff on your pass line bet will destroy you because you can't make up that deficit. There are many people who refuse to take odds on the 4 or 10 because it is so hard to make either of those numbers (only three ways each). They're right. They are hard to make, but you can't leave a point number of 4 or 10 sitting naked with no odds. There's a 6 to 3 edge against you getting your point, and even if it does hit, you get a lousy even-money payoff.

The reason those people don't take odds on the 4 or 10 is because they are playing with a short or scared bankroll. When you play short, you play scared. When you play scared, you play stupid. When you play stupid, you lose! So don't play short. By not playing short, you'll bet properly, which includes taking odds when you bet the pass line.

For whatever reason, if you aren't going to take odds, then *don't play the pass line.* Just use place betting, which is what I told you way back in the beginning of this book. Were you listening? No? Will you listen now? Let's hope so.

Let's go on to the question heading this section: "Should you lay odds?" In my humble opinion, the answer is: you should not lay odds on your don't bets. You're giving back the edge you had when you established your point. I will repeat that message: you're giving back the edge you had when you established your point. Read that again and again. Now let's look at what it means.

You put $5 on the don't pass and silently pray that the shooter does not throw a 7 or 11, which would gobble up your bet. God hears your prayers, and the shooter sets 10 as his point. Now you're in fat city. You avoided that dreaded 7 or 11 on the come-out roll and established a 10 as your point, where you have six ways of winning (the 7) and three ways of losing (4-6, 6-4, 5-5). The odds are overwhelmingly in your favor.

You're risking $5 to win $5 with the chances of winning 2 to 1 in your favor. If you decide to lay the correct odds on that $5 don't pass bet, it would cost you $10 to win an additional $5 (2 to 1 lay of odds).

Now you're risking $15 to win $10. You've gone from $5 to win $5 to giving $15 to win $10. You've watered down your dollar edge. My opinion is that you do not lay odds for the sake of picking up an additional amount of your original bet. When you get to the chapter "Money Management," however, you'll see examples where you do lay odds, but just for one roll of the dice and strictly to protect an additional don't come bet. This will all be explained in Chapter 4.

For now, understand what it means to lay odds and whether it is best to do so. My opinion is: *No!* What's yours?

LAYING AGAINST THE NUMBER

This is a form of wrong, or don't, betting, whereby you want to choose the number you're going to bet against. By coming through the don't come, you must take the number that is rolled. The main thing to understand about handling the placing and laying of numbers is that the rules differ, as illustrated below:

- You *can* place the 4, 5, 9, and 10 for any increments of $5 and up. For example, you can place the 5 for just $5 (at a $5-minimum table, obviously).
- You *cannot* lay against any of those numbers for $5.
- You *can* place the 6 and 8 for the table minimum. For example, you can place either of these for $6 each.
- You *cannot* lay against the 6 or 8 for $6.

The casinos allow small place bets when you are betting "right." That's because they have the 7 working for them and it gives them an edge over any number. If you are betting against a number (called laying against a number), there is a minimum that you must bet. The minimum bet is the amount it costs you to win $20. Since a unit is considered a $5 bet, you must bet enough of a lay for you to win $20 (four units).

Let's suppose you wanna lay against a number by *not* going through the don't pass line or the don't come box. A smart don't bettor knows how that 7 or 11 can beat him on the come-out roll, so he bypasses that bet and waits for a number to be established. Then he drops his chips on the table in the amount of the lay to win $20, plus a 5 percent charge against the $20 for the right to make that bet. He is willing to pay that 5 percent charge because he doesn't have to worry about getting beat by the 7 or 11, and he gets to choose which number he can lay against. To lay against the 4 or 10, for example, he drops $41 on the table and says, "Forty-one no-four please." That's $41 to win $20, the true 2 to 1 odds versus the 4, plus the extra dollar, which is 5 percent of the potential $20 win.

Read that last paragraph again and again, as it explains the power of the lay for don't bettors and allows them to pick their lay number. Here are the amounts of the dollar lay versus each individual number:

Number	True Odds	Lay Plus 5 Percent
4	2–1 (6–3)	$40 plus $1
5	3–2 (6–4)	$30 plus $1
6	6–5 (6–5)	$24 plus $1
8	6–5 (6–5)	$24 plus $1
9	3–2 (6–4)	$30 plus $1
10	2–1 (6–3)	$40 plus $1

You can take your lay bet down any time you wish. One thing I should mention here is that while the usual minimum lay is set at four units (to win $20), there are some Vegas and Native American casinos that will let you lay increments of two units (to win $10). In those cases, you are required to lay $11 to win $10. That's a 10 percent vig, but it does reduce the amount of the money you need to invest. This is not a bad way to play. The main thing to understand about this move is that you don't have to worry about fighting the 7 or 11 to establish a don't number, and you get to choose which numbers you want to lay against. The downside is that you must lay the true odds, but in the long run, getting away from that 7 or 11 on the come-out is a big plus for don't bettors!

- Don't come bet (X) is placed behind the number it applies to.
- If you lay against a number (Example ✔ on no-9), your bet is placed in this box.

Notice that the same box is used for a don't come bet and a lay bet, because they are both "against" a number. Chips are placed according to where that player is standing at that table.

The following illustration will give you an idea of where the don't come bets are placed. The players who lay against the number have their chips positioned in the same section:

X NO FOUR   ✔ NO NINE

X				✔	
		PLACE ┼ BETS			
4	**5**	**SIX**	**8**	**NINE**	**10**
		PLACE ┼ BETS			

THE FIELD

Turn back to the layout and you'll see the field sitting right in front—large enough to grab your attention. The house edge is about 5.56 percent, which means it ain't the best play on the table, but it sure ain't the worst. Here is some basic information on the field:

- It is a one-roll action bet.
- The minimum is $5 (or the amount of that particular table).
- A bet can be made on the come-out roll.
- Winning numbers are 2, 3, 4, 9, 10, 11, or 12. Numbers 2 and 12 pay double (2 to 1).

- Some houses pay triple (3 to 1) on the 12, reducing the vig to approximately 2.70.

My friend, Ken E. Kount, is a math genius, and right away he screams out, "Hey, I can win with more numbers than I can lose with. I'm gonna mortgage my house on this bet." While he's fumbling for his house deed, let me show you why this guy is in left field without a glove. To be sure, there are more numbers that can produce a win than the four numbers that will beat you (5, 6, 7, or 8).

The winners are 2, 3, 4, 9, 10, 11, and 12. Since seven numbers are better than four, the initial thought is to play the field, but to truly figure out what type of edge you have, you must count the ways that each number can be made.

The Losers

5: four ways	7: six ways
6: five ways	8: five ways

Those four numbers can be made twenty ways, the strongest edge against you.

The Winners

2: one way	10: three ways
3: two ways	11: two ways
4: three ways	12: one way
9: four ways	

That's sixteen ways of winning, as opposed to twenty ways of losing. I'll even give you an additional two ways of winning, because the 2 and 12 pay double. That's still 20 to 18 against you.

It's not like playing in the traffic at rush hour on the Los Angeles freeway but at least with the field, you have a chance of surviving. With the Los Angeles freeway, if the traffic doesn't get you, the earthquakes will.

The field is not a great bet, but not a bad one, either. It's somewhere in between, because you could catch streaks. The next chapter gives you moves.

BETTING THE FIELD

In gambling, trends dominate. I mentioned this in the Little Three section, but you may have forgotten it. Being able to zero in on trends and take advantage of them is a powerful edge for players. The field is subject to trends often happening both for and against the player. I advise checking the trends and waiting for a field number to show. Then you bet the field and continue betting the field until a loss occurs. Then you do not bet again until a field number shows.

Let's say the sequence of numbers at a table was 4, 9, 5, 5, 11, 4, 11, 3, 9, and 7 out. That was a double hit, two losses, and then five fields in a row. I will play "follow the field" for the next shooter because the trend is toward field numbers. Suppose he establishes 9 as his point, which is a field number. Because a field number showed, you now bet the field. Let's say the number was 4, another winner. Bet the field again. Suppose a 6 shows next. You lose. You stop and don't bet the field again until a winning number appears, then you bet the field. This is called following the field.

In the next section, you will see a system called the regression system, which could be used in playing the field. It will be explained in detail, so I won't go into it now, but just remember that you can use that here.

When following the field (another term for following the trend), the theory is very simple:

1. When a field number shows, bet the field.
2. Continue betting the field until a loss occurs.
3. Do not make another field bet until the 2, 3, 4, 9, 10, 11, or 12 shows, triggering your start of a new series of bets.
4. If you lose three times in a row, whereby a field number

showed, you made a bet and then lost: *Stop betting at that table on the field.*

5. Don't follow the field until you see a majority of field numbers appearing during the course of play.

Is this a good or bad bet? It ain't like waking up and finding a movie beauty next to you, but it's better than a stick in the eye!

WRAPPING UP KNOWLEDGE

We're coming to the end of what I consider the least important part of the book, yet it is the second part of the Big Four: knowledge. Did I cover everything? I hope so, but grab the page that contains the layout and we'll quickly scan the whole table.

- **Any Seven** Don't you dare play it.
- **Come** A bad bet, but we already said that.
- **Don't Come** This is in the same family as the don't pass and should be reviewed if you're a "wrong" bettor.
- **Don't Pass** There are a lot of sections on don't betting methods, but this was definitely covered.
- **E and C** Obviously *E* is for "11" and *C* is for "craps." Just remember that the stick man puts your bets on the layout (next to the arrows) pointing to where you are standing. They are one-roll bets.
- **Field** Just explained it. See the section, "Betting the Field."
- **Odds** Not shown, but they come into play *after* the point is established.
- **Pass Line** Yes, this was done, but just remember that if you want to throw the dice, you have to have a bet on the pass line or don't pass line.
- **Place Betting** This is the way to play and the most important phase of craps. We'll go over some betting moves in the next section. Be sure you understand place bets.

- **Proposition Bets**   This was definitely covered. Hard way bets are not a bad move, but the one-roll bets, such as any craps and yo (11), should only be used as hedge bets.

Well, it seems we covered everything. Good. Now we can move on to the real meat: money management. If you aren't clear on a specific topic, leaf back and go over that section.

4

Money Management

If you are new to gambling, then you're the perfect person to grasp this sentence: "The whole key to winning at gambling is money management and discipline." There ain't nothin' else.

This section covers the money management of gambling, and without this all-important skill, your time at the tables will be short. So what is money management? I could tell you it is guts, brains, control, maneuvering, decisions, and on and on, but let's make it simple: Money management is knowing what to bet when you win and what to bet when you lose. Sounds simple, but can you do it? Based on the millions of people who gamble every day and drop their wads of cash on the table, it's evident that people don't know how to manage their chips. This will be explained in detail on these pages, though it may go in one ear, roll around a bit, and pop out the other side.

My personal opinion on how to gamble is: very conservatively. You can either buy that theory or come up with your own, but at least take a look at my moves. I know everything there is to know about craps, but so do thousands of other people. What separates me from them is how I control my bets. Way back in the section on

bankroll, we went over sessions, series, win goals, and loss limits—all
designed to show you how to control your money. Obviously, all that
is part of money management, but the coup de grace of betting is
predetermining a method and then following it to the nth degree.

I gamble the way grass grows—slowly and methodically. I've been
gambling since politicians were honest (yes, that long!). The thing
that got me winning was zeroing in on a sensible conservative style
and sticking with it. When you become a perfect player and start
popping out winning sessions 60 to 65 percent of the time, you can
write your own book with your own theories. Until then, take a look
at the upcoming topics.

DO YOU WANT MONEY MANAGEMENT?

Yes and no. Yes, you want it because you feel it will make you a
winner. No, because you feel it's too restrictive and will control your
chances of getting the big kill. A professional gambler, if he really is a
serious player, learns over and over that you rarely get the gold ring
of untold bonanzas and that you should settle for small consistent
returns.

It took me a long, long, long time to accept small returns. I don't
win every day, but when I lose, the loss limits I set up restrict the
amount of my setback. There are win goals that are set with realistic
amounts, and coming home with small profits sure beats those long
rides home with big dreams gone astray and empty pockets
reminding me that I didn't have the brains to quit. On those days, I
didn't want money management because I wanted the sweet smell of
success, which was only measured by the amount of the score. It
didn't happen enough. So, what's a boob like me gonna do? I wrote
down my options:

1. Acquire money management.
2. Get a job.

Since I detest anything that requires effort for accomplishment, I chose number one—reluctantly. Now it is too late to go back to being a dork. I crave the big hit, the untold riches, but that only happens in the movies.

Whether or not you want to learn money management, it behooves you to realize right up front that without it, you don't have a prayer of winning consistently. This is my basic premise to gambling and is echoed by other pros. Remember: "It doesn't matter how much you win! It matters how little you lose!"

THE REGRESSION SYSTEM

This is my system. I first banged it out in 1984 in my first blackjack book. I've been using it ever since New York was a prairie, and I love it. It's conservative, but it works. In my book *Advanced Craps,* I went over this method. If you read that book, you'll notice the similarity, but why would you read *Advanced Craps* before this book?

Here is the regression system, repeated for your reading pleasure. First, a big reminder: the book you are reading is for the clueless craps player. I'm including an excerpt on the regression system from *Advanced Craps,* which goes deeper into money management. Read on.

In 1984, I wrote a book on blackjack that explained this method of betting. I believe it is hands-down the most powerful approach to money management ever put out. It is primarily aimed at "even" bets, such as blackjack, baccarat, the outside bets of roulette, sports betting, 6 and 8 in craps, and the don't pass line, excluding odds. If you don't know the theory by now, you should hang your head low, but just for smiles, I'll go over it again, because it's gonna get a lot of play in my systems. I apply the regression theory to most of my betting moves. Why? Because it works!

The basic idea is to bet higher than the minimum, and after a win *regress* down to the minimum, thereby wrapping up a profit. That means you can win one bet in a series and yet be guaranteed a profit. The key to the system is the second bet, whereby you regress the next wager.

You must always bet higher than the table minimum in order to give yourself room to go down, and the amount of that first bet is based on your bankroll. I'll start by giving you the method as it pertains to $5 increments.

You're at a $5 blackjack table, so your first bet is $10. If you win, the dealer slides $10 profit to you, and you've got $20 in front of you. Here's the key move: Take back the $10 you started with, plus $5 of the winning payoff, and bet $5. At this point, you're in fat city. You've got your original $10 back, plus a profit of $5, and even if you lose the next bet, your series shows a $5 profit.

After a win, most people bet the same amount or go up one unit (a $5 bet) or even two. If a loss occurs on that second bet, they're in a position where they won a bet, lost a bet, and are either even or, heavens to Betsy, out a unit or two. Yet they won just as many hands as the house. My regression system has you winning for that series— even though you won only *one* hand.

Four guys walk up to a $5 table, and each bets $10. Each wins his bet, yet each has a different theory as to what the next bet should be:

1. Player A pulls back $10 profit and bets $10.
2. Player B pulls back $5 and bets $15.
3. Player C pulls back nothing and bets $20.
4. Player D pulls back $15 and bets $5.

Let's say they all lose the next hand. Look at the results:

1. Player A won a hand, lost a hand, and he's even.

2. Player B won a hand, lost a hand, and he's out $5 even though he played the house even. (Each won one hand.)

3. Player C won a hand, lost a hand, and is out $10 even though he won as many hands as the house. (Each won one hand.)

4. Player D ends up with a $5 profit, even though both he and the house won one hand.

Once the profit is locked into that series, you can become aggressive with your wagers. For instance, you win that second bet of $5. The dealer slides a $5 chip over to you and you let the whole $10 ride, fully aware of the fact that the series bet is in a profit lock.

Suppose you win that third bet of $10. At this point, you revert to "up and pull," a powerful method of money management that has a couple of sections dedicated to it a little later on in this chapter.

Anyway, you win the bet at $10 and incorporate the up and pull theory. Raise your bet "up" to $15 and "pull" back a profit of $5, which further increases the previous profit for the series, which was gleaned by regressing after the first win. If that $15 bet also wins, you now go up to $20 and pull back $10. You could have gone up to $25 and pulled back $5, and that is strictly up to you. Naturally, I would have you go up only $5, but then, I like the conservative approach.

It is important to remember: every winning bet must give you a profit, so don't think you can raise the subsequent bet by the full amount of the win. Every winning bet must result in a profit being pulled back!

Stop right here, my friend, and go back over that last paragraph. It was meant for every single solitary one of you, and it should be memorized backwards and forwards.

When you get into your series, be absolutely sure you take back a profit after *every* winning score. I cannot stress enough the power of this approach or the necessity of it. Guys like Imus Pressit and Y. R.

Kash, Frank Lee Board, I. M. Madork, and P. Weebrane will scoff at this theory and claim you can't win serious money by being conservative. All I'm asking is that you give up that second winning bet in a series, lock up a profit, and then aggressively increase your bets. Besides, what's so hard about taking back a profit after each winning hand or roll? I'm still letting you increase your bets. All I'm asking is that you take back a profit. You'll get more of this in the section "Up and Pull," so let's finish the regression theory.

As you continue to win, you can raise your bets as long as each win results in a profit being stashed. Naturally, you can also insert another regression into your series, and the smarter players will want to do that. It just means you lock up a bigger profit at a specific time in your series, and then start back up.

Let's finish that winning series you were in. You won at $15 and had the option of going to either $20 or $25. We'll say you went to $20. Suppose you win again and the dealer slides $20 over to you. This time you get a little more aggressive and raise the bet to $35 while pulling back $5. You get another winning hand and the dealer slides $35 over to you. At this point, you slap another regression bet into your series. Take back the $35 and regress your bet:

1. All the way down to $10.
2. Partially to $20.
3. Partially to $25.
4. One unit ($5) to $30.

Choose any of the above, and you can't go wrong. Then you can start back up. For instance, Connie Conservative drops her next bet all the way down to $10 and each subsequent winning hand is increased by $5. I love her!

Aggie Aggressive likes the regression but drops her next bet to $30, and every succeeding win is pulled back with another $5 lopped off her bet. For instance, she wins at $30 and then bets $25. Then she wins at $25 and drops to $20, leaving less money at risk.

The variations go on and on. An upcoming section will give you tables to follow, but of course, you could come up with your own. Just remember that after a loss, you revert back to the beginning bet of the series and start over.

I might just warn you, or maybe you know already: you aren't gonna win forever, so you better think about incorporating second regressions into your series. It will soften the blow when that inevitable loss does occur.

I've talked a lot about the regression, and this was a chatty section but a necessary one. There is also a method of betting called off-amounts, that come into play at the blackjack and roulette tables, but not in craps, so I won't explain it here. Some time ago, I released a book entitled *So You Wanna be a Gambler: Advanced Roulette*. It covers "off amounts" and four chapters on regression and a bellyful of theories on betting according to this method. It wouldn't hurt you to spring for the book, and it would give you a firm grip on this tremendous betting method. The game may be roulette, but the theory on betting is the same.

I don't care if you think I'm trying to sell a book. I'm trying to get you to fully understand the whole concept of betting, even as it applies to other games that have no bearing on craps. Since you should be keyed in on the regression system about now, swing right into the next chapter and take a look at some series.

REGRESSION SERIES

To continue to explain this theory of betting, here is another excerpt from my *Advanced Craps*. This will give you a good look at different betting series. Since you will be getting a lot of series for the handling of the 6 and 8, I won't go into that here, but I do want to give you an idea of "running series" in blackjack or roulette in order to acquaint you fully with the method.

$5 Table

	A	B	C	D	E
First bet	$10	$8	$8	$10	$10
Second bet	$5	$5	$5	$5	$5
Third bet	$8	$7	$7	$8	$10
Fourth bet	$10	$11	$10	$12	$15
Fifth bet	$5	$15	$10	$17	$15
Sixth bet	$8	$10	$15	$25	$20
Seventh bet	$10	$25	$15	$25	$25

Some of those series have double regressions and all stop at $25 as the max (5 times the minimum).

$10 Table

	A	B	C	D	E
First bet	$15	$15	$20	$20	$20
Second bet	$10	$10	$10	$10	$10
Third bet	$15	$10	$15	$15	$15
Fourth bet	$25	$20	$20	$25	$20
Fifth bet	$35	$25	$30	$45	$15
Sixth bet	$45	$20	$40	$25	$20
Seventh bet	$50	$15	$50	$45	$30

You have more room for various series as the betting increments increase, but the $10 table should also have five times your table minimum as your maximum bet ($50) until you reach your win goal. This will be explained later.

$25 Table

	A	B	C	D	E
First bet	$35	$40	$50*	$50	$40
Second bet	$25	$25	$25*	$25	$25
Third bet	$35	$30	$35	$30	$30
Fourth bet	$50	$50	$60	$50	$50
Fifth bet	$75	$60	$90	$75	$70
Sixth bet	$100	$100	$90	$100	$50
Seventh bet	$125	$100	$60	$75	$75

*You could go to a $5 table and make the first bet $30 and the second $5 to have a spread of $25 in your profit regress. This would hold down your risk factor from $50 to $30 in the event you lose your first bet. So don't think you must go to a $25 table to get a $25 spread. This can be done at the lower tables.

$100 Table

	A	B	C	D	E
First bet	$150	$150	$200	$200	$150
Second bet	$100	$100	$100	$100	$100
Third bet	$125	$150	$150	$150	$150
Fourth bet	$150	$200	$200	$250	$200
Fifth bet	$200	$300	$350	$150	$300
Sixth bet	$250	$400	$500	$250	$200
Seventh bet	$300	$500	$400	$150	$300

Naturally, you'll come up with your own variations, but just remember to regress after the first win, and it ain't a bad idea to incorporate another regression move in your series. You might feel somebody will think you're a cheapskate for using a double regression, but I have a scoop for you. More people will think you're a sharp cat—and I'll be the first one to pat you on the back.

You should now have a complete grasp of the regression method. If you don't, go back and read the last two chapters before going on.

WHAT IS MONEY MANAGEMENT?

Don't tell me you can't answer that question, because it's the key to whether you win or lose. The previous sections went over a method whereby you lock up a profit after only *one* win. The key is your ability and guts to take back your original bet, with a profit and a guarantee of a win for that series, regardless of the amount. Sure, it's gonna be hard, because you want to get that big return, but if you get in the habit of accepting small returns, you will cut your chances of suffering big losses and avoid the depression that goes with losing.

In the first chapter, you learned how to play the game of craps. Now you will learn how to bet at craps, so as to point you toward winning days while holding down your losses. We'll go over simple systems that will get you started, and then you can add your own theories.

I play craps all the time at the casinos but strictly on the place bets. That is the easiest and surest way to get the numbers you want because you get to choose, but since most craps players love to throw the dice, the next section gives you a look at betting the pass line. Read it, but reserve judgment on whether you'll play the pass line until after you've finished the sections on place betting. What is money management? You mean you still don't know?

PASS LINE PLAY

No, I don't play the pass line, even when it's my turn to shoot. I don't play the pass line for three very good reasons:

- I wanna pick my own numbers on which to bet.

- I don't want the 4 or 10.
- I wanna come down and come off whenever I choose.

Keep in mind that when the shooter establishes a point, the average number of rolls he will throw until he sevens-out or makes his point is three. That's all—three. Sure, the shooter might throw a few craps and 11s, but only three numbers, which result in payoffs for the "right" bettors, is all you can hope for. All serious craps players know this, yet at the table they never say the three magic words: Take me down.

Okay, you're playing the pass line and have $5 on the table. The shooter establishes a 10 as his point. Since you always want the 6 and 8 as part of your roll (since these are the prime numbers for the "right" bettor), here's what you do as soon as the point is set:

1. Take single odds.
2. Place the 6 and 8 for $6 each.

That's it. Even if the 4, 5, or 9 was your point, always take single odds and place the 6 and the 8 for $6 each. If the 6 was your point, take single odds and place the 8. If the 8 was your point, take single odds and place the 6.

If your pass line bet was $10, then take single odds and place the 6 and 8 for $12 each. Make the amount of your place bets the same unit increments as your original pass line bet. If the 6 becomes the point and you have $5 on the line:

- Take single odds and place the 8 and 5 for single units each (a unit is $5 for all place bets, except for the 6 and 8, which are $6 bets).
- Place double units if your pass line bet is two units.

If 8 becomes the point and you have $5 on the line:

- Take single odds and place the 6 and 9 for single units.

- Place double units if your pass line bet is two units.

Notice that you always end up with your pass line bet with odds, plus the all-powerful 6 and 8.

Just to be consistent, I suggest you place the lower number 5 when 6 is the point and the higher number 9 when 8 is the point. If a 7 shows on the come-out roll, you get paid for your pass line bet (we'll say it's $5). Do *not* let the whole $10 ride, as most players do. That means you have to put up two chips as odds when the point is established, causing you to load up too much on an initial roll. If the 7 shows on the come-out, take the profit and let your original bet stand. (Read this again, all of you "press it" players.) If the shooter sevens-out before making a point, start over again with the same bet for the next shooter.

Go back and digest this section. Here it is in a nutshell, if you are a pass line player (remember: a unit is a $5 bet, except when placing the 6 and 8, which are $6 bets.):

1. One-unit pass line bet:
   a. If the point is 4, 5, 9, or 10, take single odds and place the 6 and 8 for single units.
   b. If the point is 6, take single odds and place the 5 and 8 for single units.
   c. If the point is 8, take single odds and place the 6 and 9 for single units.
   d. If any craps (2, 3, or 12) shows, you lose the $5 pass line bet. come back with just a $5 pass line bet.
   e. If 7 or 11 shows on a come-out roll, you win $5. Make the same $5 bet. Do *not* go up to $10.
2. Two-unit ($10) pass line bet:
   a. If the point is 4, 5, 9, or 10, take single odds and place the 6 and 8 for $12 each.
   b. If the point is 6, take single odds and place the 5 and 8 for double units.

    c. If the point is 8, take single odds and place the 6 and 9 for double units.

Could it be simpler? My friend, Simm Pulton says yes. He would!

PASS LINE INCREASES

Someday you'll realize that "this white man does not speak with forked tongue." This has to do with my conservative theory and trying to get you to avoid getting whacked.

Craps players are crazy bettors, always banging up their bets, looking for the kill. They take the maximum odds offered at the table, but they never think of the possibility of losing, so they constantly increase their bets. I think differently.

Let's suppose you're betting $5 with single odds and the shooter makes his point. I do not jump my pass line bet to $10 because by taking odds, there is the chance that if I lose that second game, I end up a loser for that shooter, even though I won one game and lost one game. You'll eventually get chewed up. If the shooter makes that first point and you have a single-unit bet and single odds, my next come-out bet is a single unit, and I take double odds behind the line. This way you hold down potential losses.

Let's say the shooter makes that second point and you win that single-unit bet with double odds. The amount of the next come-out is $10, and you take double odds. You then make double-unit place bets on the 6 and 8. If the point was 6 or 8, you'd place double-unit bets on the 5 or 9 (see the previous section).

You've heard the old saying, "There ain't no such thing as a free lunch." Well, in craps, there ain't no such thing as a red-hot roll without it's drawback. If you keep raising your bets without taking profits, eventually the 7 takes you down, along with the stacks of chips you left riding on the table.

If you catch a shooter who is making a ton of pass line numbers, here is my suggestion for your pass line bets, based on starting with one unit ($5). The following example is based on the shooter continuing to make his pass line bet.

First bet: single-unit pass line, single odds, single place bets.
Second bet: single-unit pass line, double odds, double place bets.
Third bet: double-unit pass line, double odds, double place bets.
Fourth bet: triple-unit pass line, triple odds, triple place bets.
Fifth bet: double-unit place bets, double odds, double place bets.

After the third bet, which is a pass line win, you could stay at double units instead of triple units. Often on the fifth bet is when you could go back to double-unit pass line, double odds, and double place bets. The choices vary, but don't keep raising your bets without sticking in a regression move somewhere along the line. Sure it's conservative, but, if you have a small session bankroll and start off with single-unit bets, you should be thankful to get a couple of pass line wins, plus some place number payoffs. Just don't leave your profits on the table, as so many players do.

PLACE BETTING

Since the beginning of time, people have written books on how to play craps. Go ahead, buy a few dozen of them and you'll notice they all tell you to do the same thing: bet the pass line, take maximum odds, and take two come bets, also with maximum odds.

Well, they've been building casinos with craps tables for many years, and still nobody has broken the house.

I don't intend for you to try and break the house, but I already saved you the $387 you would have spent on all those other books by giving you their main method. Think back to the example about choosing the number you would like to get as your point. Most everyone would scream 6 and 8, and they'd be right, but since there are ten ways to make the 6 and 8, and fourteen ways to make the 4, 5, 9, or 10, the odds of you getting the point you want is 14 to 10 against you.

Here is what you should do:

1. Bypass the come-out roll.
2. Regardless of what number becomes the point, place the 6 and 8.
3. You get the 6 and 8 as your numbers 100 percent of the time.

We'll assume you're a $5 bettor with a $100 session amount:

1. Bypass the come-out roll. (Notice you do this most of the time.)
2. Place the 6 and 8 for $6 each.
3. Take one hit on either the 6 or 8 and come off both bets.
4. You've got a $7 profit for that game.

In the last example, be aware that the average number of numbers to be thrown after the point is established is three, and you are coming down after only one hit.

All of the following examples are based on what you do after a point is established and you have *no* bets on the pass line:

1. Place the 6 and 8 for $6 each.
2. Take two hits on any combination of the 6 and 8.
3. Take both bets down.

In this last example, after you place your first bet, you have $7 in hand, with $12 on the board. The worst you could lose is $5, but if the shooter bangs another 6 or 8, you win $7 more. You are risking $5 to win $14.

Next example, $100 Session amount:

1. Place the 6 and 8 for $12 each.
2. After the first hit, regress both bets to $6 each.
3. Take one more hit on either the 6 or 8 and take both bets down.

Look at that again. After you get a payoff of $14 with the first win, you come down to risk $12 against a $14 payoff. You're in a no-lose situation. You either get one more hit on the 6 or 8 and bring both bets off, giving you a profit of $21, or the shooter sevens-out after that first hit and you still have a profit of $2.

This is what I want you to base your play on. The regression off of the first hit puts you in fat city. Naturally, the risk on the table to get that first hit is $24, but in gambling you are *always* risking money. My theory has you risking this money for very, very short periods of time, but if you can't stand *any* heat, get out of the kitchen.

A personal note: This is the section that I want all of you beginners to zero in on. The messages I have been giving you all lead to this way of playing. Before moving on, go back and review these basic steps.

TWENTY-TWO INSIDE

The previous chapter had you starting only with the 6 and 8. You could take either one hit or two hits and then come off. The one I like best is $12 each on the 6 and 8, regressing to $6 each after one hit and putting yourself in a no-lose situation—or have I said that before?

Now we move $22 inside, which is simply $5 on both the 5 and 9, and $6 on both the 6 and 8. For you nonbelievers, "22" is the name of the bet.

Continuing with examples, all variations on bypassing the come-out roll, let's look at the basic move:

1. Place $22 inside.
2. After the first hit, take down the 5 and 9.
3. Take one more hit on the 6 or 8 and take both down.

In the above example, you are risking $22 on the initial bet, but you have four numbers working with a total of eighteen ways to make those four numbers versus the six ways for the 7 to beat you. That's 3 to 1 in your favor.

By taking the 5 and 9 down after the first hit, you reduce your potential loss to $12, minus the $7 you collected, for a total $5 loss. Look at the upside: after only one hit with $22 inside and taking down the 5 and 9, the worst you could lose is $5, although another score with the 6 or 8 leaves you risking $5 to win $14.

Some of you will leave the $22 inside bet up after the first hit to give you another shot with eighteen ways to make those four numbers. In that case, you could lose $15 to win $14, rather than risk $5 to win $14. I prefer my first method, removing the 5 and 9.

One more tidbit: Some of you may want to leave that string of $22 inside working for the duration of that shooter's roll. I disagree. You need three hits on those numbers to cover the $22 at risk, and you'll soon learn to realize the power of that 7 staring you in the face.

Again, my suggestion is to accept small returns. This can only be accomplished by learning how to cut potential losses and grabbing those small returns when you can. This is another powerful starting point for beginners. Go back over this section again.

TAKE ME DOWN

Don't skip this section! Don't scoff at this advice! This topic, along with win goals, loss limits, accepting small returns, and minimizing losses, are the most important tips you will get from me.

Memorize these three words and get used to saying them: "Take me down." You probably won't or can't do this. Craps players have the biggest egos of any player in the casino. They are looked upon (usually by themselves) as the macho group of gamblers. At the craps table, you'll hear all types of yelling, screaming, and encouragement for the shooter. In other words, you have the license to act like a jerk. You rarely hear the screams at the blackjack, baccarat, or roulette tables. Those players lose too, but they do it in silence.

I once saw a blackjack player call for the dealer to hit his two up-cards of 2 and 2 against her Jack. In order, she gave him a 4, 2, 3, 2,

Ace, and a 6, and he broke with a 22. He didn't scream, holler, or curse, but you know he was boiling when he lost, though he tried not to show it. He had a pen in his hand that he snapped in two, spraying ink on everyone around him.

If you see a guy walking around with an ink-stained sweater—he's the guy who doesn't show his emotions, but if he were at a craps table, he could punch out the little old lady next to him and get away with it.

Let's get back to the three magic words: "Take me down." When you say these words, you're telling the dealer to bring your place bets down (off). Since there are so many macho players at the craps table, you'll get a few stares or comments such as:

"You're never gonna get the big kill by coming off."
"What are you afraid of?"
"You're too conservative."

Deep in their hearts, though, there are many, many players who want to take their bets down but are too intimidated to tell the dealer. It takes brains, guts, nerve, or whatever you want to call it, to get a couple of scores and cut the possibility of losing back the profits. Eventually that 7 will pop up, and the players who have a ton of bets on the layout die a little, as the dealer scoops up their chips.

I preach money management and discipline. The biggest step that you'll take at craps will be to memorize these words: "Take me down."

FORTY-FOUR INSIDE

We're gonna move up to my own favorite way of playing when starting the day, but this example will involve the highest monetary risk we'll discuss. The power of this move is that it covers the four inside numbers for a total of eighteen combinations that could occur against that dreaded 7, which can be made six ways. It gives you a powerful 3 to 1 edge, but remember, the risk is $44 on that single roll.

The other strong point with this system is the guaranteed profit looming after only one hit. Here's the play:

1. Bypass the come-out roll.
2. Regardless of which number is the point, place $44 inside, $10 each on the 5 and 9, and $12 each on the 6 and 8.
3. After the first hit, which gives you a $14 payoff, regress all bets to $6 on the 6 and $6 on the 8. This means you take the 5 and 9 off.
4. Wait for one more hit on either the 6 or 8 and take both bets down.

With $44 inside, you have four numbers that will kick off $14. By regressing to $6 each on the 6 and 8, you are in a no-lose situation because you have $14 in your rack and only $12 on the board.

Even a seven-out leaves you with a $2 profit, but another 6 or 8 gives you an additional $7. That means you win either $2 or $21. There is an option to $44 inside, which I'll show you in the event you are a tad aggressive:

1. Bypass the come-out roll.
2. Place $44 inside.
3. After the first hit, go to $22 inside.
4. One more hit and all bets off.

In this case, after you get your $14 score, you leave $22 on the board.

- The good part: you have four numbers instead of two (18 to 10) working for that second hit.
- The bad part: after the first payoff of $14, you have $22 at risk, meaning you could lose $8 if the 7 shows, even though you have eight extra combinations working for you (the eight total combinations of making the 5 and 9).

Choose your method. My choice is $6 on the 6 and 8 and a no-lose situation. Obviously, there are dozens of spin-offs, starting with various combinations of bets, but this book is aimed at the novice player, and I have no intention of trying to impress you with too many variables. Still, I strongly urge you to read my *Advanced Craps* (*Basic Craps* is optional) to pick up a ton of offshoots.

One more note: most of my plays do not include pass line bets. They are geared to place bets and regression bets—or have you already noticed?

CHARTING THE TABLES

When I first went on TV back in 1984, I would concentrate each week on telling the callers and audience the importance of "charting the tables." For those of you who think I'm referring to charting the stars or charting a course, you're off base. Charting, as it pertains to craps, means that you predetermine which way you want to bet ("right" or "wrong"). You chart the tables to find a game going in the direction you want to play.

Sometimes it will take you hours to find a table going the way you predetermined your betting and then an opening at that table. So what? Don't you want to be sure you're betting "right" at a hot table and betting "wrong" at a cold table?

My friend, I. M. Madork, is a confirmed do ("right") bettor. He'll walk into a casino and rush up to the first table he finds that has an opening. He has no idea which way the trend in that game is going. He may get stuck at a frigid table.

I refuse to go to any table, or any game, without charting. What should you look for? If you're a "right" bettor, you want two games where the shooter establishes a point and throws at least one 6 or 8, or two games where the shooter establishes a point and throws at least one inside number, before sevening-out or making his point.

Regardless of whether you're playing the inside numbers or the 6 and 8, you're looking for inside numbers. Suppose you're charting a table and a guy sets his point and throws twenty-seven numbers before he makes his point. He is scorching. He comes out to establish a new point and gets an 8 but sevens-out on the next roll. Even though he had a red-hot roll prior to that, it was not two games in a row. You have to stop and start all over, waiting for two games in a row, even though it's two different shooters.

Remember, you're not betting the point, you're betting the numbers. If you're betting the pass line, the charting procedure is the shooter makes two points in a row; 7 or 11 on the come-out roll does not count as a point. If the shooter makes two consecutive points, then buy in and start betting the pass line, even on that same shooter.

Back to charting place numbers. We'll say a shooter establishes a point of 9 and throws 6, 5, 3, 8, 6, and sevens-out. That counts as one good roll because you would have won betting the place numbers. The next shooter sets 8 as his point and throws 6, 5, and sevens-out. You still would have won if you were playing. Even though two shooters in a row sevened-out, the place bettors would have won. You can play at that table.

The next section goes into the key points that keep you at a table after charting gets you into a game. Is charting important? What do you think?

KEY NUMBER: THREE

The importance of setting loss limits at a table is absolutely imperative. You simply have to set a limit to the amount of money you will lose. My suggestion is 50 percent, but as you climb into higher starting-session amounts, the percentage should drop. Here are a few suggestions, based on your starting-session amount:

- Up to $500 session: 50 percent loss limit.
- $600 to $1,000 session: 40 percent loss limit.
- $1,000 to $2,000 session: 30 percent loss limit.

You can vary the percentages, but keep 50 percent as the maximum loss limit. Don't be afraid to pack it in if you're being ground out and your losses reach even 20 or 25 percent. There are dozens of tables to choose from, so why stand there and get hammered when utopia might be waiting at the next table?

Enter the number three. If you have three games in succession in which the shooter establishes a number and sevens-out, you wrap up that session, period! This is your protection when you're at a choppy table, winning a few, losing a few, but seeing your session money diminish.

There is one exception to this rule. For you super-conservative players, like me, you drop to the number two. If *two* consecutive shooters establish a point and seven-out, you're done. Period. Pick two or three losses in a row to dictate your leaving that table. I choose two, but the choice is yours.

There's another time when the three comes into play. It has to do with the regression system—when you regress your bet after a hit. Let's say you're playing $44 inside and you get a hit and regress to $6 on 6 and 8. You wait for three rolls, regardless of what they are. If there is no 6 or 8, then take your bets down. I've told you this before, but it is important. There is no crime in saying it again: "Take me down!" You still end up $14 to the good.

Let me go over that last suggestion again:

1. Bypass the come-out roll.
2. Regardless of the point, play $44 inside.
3. After the first hit, when you collect $14, regress to $6 on six and $6 on 8.

At this juncture, you'll win $2 if the shooter sevens-out or $21 if he hits another 6 or 8.

But—but—but, after that first hit, however, when you collected $14 and regressed to $6 on 6 and 8, wait for only three more rolls. If the shooter does not pop another 6 or 8, take down your bets. You're still up $14. Will you do it? Maybe not, but give it some thought.

HIT AND DOWN

You've already figured out this system, so I don't have to spend a lot of time explaining it. You're looking for one hit and then you're taking your bets down. Sure, you smirk at this play, but as you get deeper into gambling, you'll find that praying for a winning day will only result in the Big Guy in the Sky telling you to use discipline and conservative plays before you call on Him.

Here is this very complicated system that you might consider using:

1. Bypass the come-out roll.
2. Place the 6 and 8 or $22 inside or $44 inside.
3. Take one hit and tell the dealer, "Take me down."

You don't have to be a rocket scientist to figure it out, but you have to want to win so bad that you'll do anything to see your chip pile grow. Technically, it is the same theory as the regression system, except that you come completely off after a score. There are many pros who love this method, but it is difficult for occasional players to implement because "they only come to play once a month, and they really don't care if they win or lose; they're only in it for fun."

I ain't gonna comment on that "don't care if I win or lose" statement, but it has to do with the reason they build stalls for donkeys. Whether or not you like the move, at least give it some thought. What's so tough about grabbing a tiny profit over and over? It's called hit and down. Someday you'll try it.

UP AND PULL

Different strokes for different folks. Everybody has their preferences. Some people like blondes, others red-heads, some brunettes. Nobody's wrong. Same goes in gambling. You might play like me (conservative) or you may prefer to be aggressive. If you're aggressive, I'll assume you'd prefer not to come off with your bets after you perform your regression, which means regressing your bets down after a hit.

The method is called up and pull, and is self-explanatory. You want to "up" your bets but "pull" back a profit after every hit, once the regression system has locked up a profit. I don't give a dingdong about the up part, but I sure want you concentrating on the pull phase. That means every time the dealer hands you a profit, make sure you pay yourself. The amount is unimportant; the difference is the deed.

Let's say you're playing $44 inside and the point is 4. The shooter throws a 5 and you collect $14, dropping your bets to $6 on 6 and 8. The shooter throws an 8 and you collect $7 but leave your bets in action. You've "pulled back" a profit.

The next roll is a 6 and you're in another $7. Here are your options:

- Same bet and take the $7.
- Add $3 and place the 5 and 9.
- Add $5 and press the 6 and 8 up to $12.

In the last two examples, you've reinvested a few dollars because that series has already locked up a profit. We'll say you go up to $12 on 6 and 8. (Remember that the regression move after the first hit made this series a no-lose proposition, so it is okay to get aggressive by adding a few dollars back.)

The shooter is on a good roll and bangs out an 8. You get $14 to play with. Your options:

- Same bet and pull back $14.
- Increase the 6 and 8 to $18 each and pull back $2.
- Take $14 and regress the 6 and 8 to $6 each.

The options are numerous, especially when you start with higher amounts. I'd strongly recommend putting in a double regression, thereby leaving less money at risk. That means the third option above would be my choice. This increases the guaranteed profit for that series.

Go back to the chapter on the regression series. Those tables are based on $5 bets and incorporate a hard and fast up and pull method.

It is somewhat difficult to implement these series on the place numbers because of one major change. At those tables, we are talking about single bets, as in blackjack, roulette, baccarat, and so forth, where there is only one bet being affected. In place betting, however, the numbers work in pairs. When you increase the 6, you must include the 8, and vice versa. When you increase the 5, you must increase the 9. They are sister numbers and work in conjunction with each other. They are increased or decreased as pairs, never separately. That's why the double regression is needed to increase your profits. At least you can incorporate the up and pull theory, however, even though you have to increase both sister numbers when you make a move.

Go back to that section on the regression series and zero in on the $10 table, just to get an idea of what I'm trying to convey. You start off regressing your $20 bet to $10, locking up a profit. Then you go up to $15 and pull back $5 after a hit. On the next hit, you increase to $20 and pull back $10. You went "up" and "pulled," and you have $20 riding. Another hit puts you in a double regression, going down to $10 and pulling back $30. The shooter is hot, you've got a nice profit, and $10 in action. On the next hit, you go up to $15 and pull back $5.

The method is called up and pull. The theory is simple. The options are staggering. They are yours. Use them.

Again, I repeat the ultra-important part of this method: The first hit *must* be a regression, and then the moves can be adjusted to your preference for an aggressive or conservative style. The higher you start your series, the more options you'll have. Finally, I am aware that the theory works best on increments of $5—$10, $15, and so forth.

In craps, the mandatory increment bets on the 6 and 8 require $6, $12, or $18, etc., but that takes only a slight adjustment on your part to work your series. Just concentrate. I live and die by the regression system and the up and pull.

GUARANTEE AND EXCESS

I have no right to yell at you people, urging you to play my way. My theories are conservative, as you'll see with this move. It's called guarantee and excess. The idea is that when you get ahead, you set aside a guaranteed profit for that session and then play with your excess.

Suppose you started with a session amount of $300 and set a win goal of 30 percent. You catch a hot streak and soon you're sitting with a $90 profit. Here's the move. Rat-hole your starting amount of $300. Take the $90 profit and split it in half. Forty-five dollars is combined with your session money and is called your guarantee: You're guaranteed to leave that table with at least a $45 profit. The other half is called your excess. Continue playing with that as long as it lasts, but you can absolutely not dip into your guarantee or session amount at that table again. No exceptions.

Every subsequent winning series is divided in half. After you split that win goal into guarantee and excess and the game resumes, let's say you win $24 on the next series. Put $12 with your guarantee and add $12 to your excess. On the next series you win $14 and split $7 to each the guarantee and excess. Your guarantee is rising and the excess, which you continue to play with, is increasing. At this point, when you are in the excess part of your win goal, you can become more aggressive with both the start of your series and the handling of your place bets, confident in the fact that you have your session money and a guaranteed profit tucked away.

How long do you stay at that table? Glad you asked. You stay there forever, bypassing dinner and trips to the john. Well, maybe I'm exaggerating, but hot tables are tough to find. How long *should* you stay? Give me a number between 2 and 4. Somebody said 3. Great! Even though my forte is gambling, I am also a whiz at math. Once I counted all the way to 7, but the teacher spotted me the 1, 2, and 3. The answer is our old friend 3. You lose three series in a row and that session is history. No excuses.

The bottom line is that many people do not have a clue as to what to do with their win goal once it is reached. The logical move is to first protect your session money by putting it aside. Then take that win goal, regardless of the amount, and rat-hole at least half of it. Now you have a guarantee and leave that session as a winner. It's up to you to explore additional conservative or even aggressive moves.

DON'T SYSTEMS

There are two ways of playing craps: do and don't (right or wrong, pass line, or don't pass line). If you play do, right, or pass line, you're looking for the shooter to make numbers while you fight that dreaded 7, which can be made six ways. If you play don't, wrong, or don't pass, you're looking for the shooter to not make numbers or points while you have that dreaded 7 working for you.

Neither method is written in stone as the best way to play. It all comes down to trends or streaks, being able to read them and then take advantage of them.

When you bet "wrong," which requires you to bet against the shooter, you are using the don't pass line on the come-out roll.

The "right" bettor has the 7 and 11 working for him on the come-out, while fighting the craps of 2, 3, or 12, which means that for one single roll the edge is 8 to 4 in favor of that "right" bettor, based on the number of ways those numbers can be made. Once the point is established, however, the odds swing away from the right bettor because that 7 can be made more ways than any other number:

- 4 or 10 (three ways): odds 2 to 1 against the shooter.
- 5 or 9 (four ways): odds 3 to 2, 6 to 4, 9 to 6 against the shooter.
- 6 or 8 (five ways): odds 6 to 5 against the shooter.

So the right bettor is constantly in fear of that 7, while the wrong bettor has it working for him once he gets past that dreaded 7 or 11 on the come-out roll. Once the point is established, the edge is clearly in favor of the don't bettor. The following outline shows you the edge the don't bettor has—once he establishes his point:

- 4 to 10 (three ways): odds 6 to 3 in favor of the wrong bettor.
- 5 or 9 (four ways): odds 6 to 4, 3 to 2, or 9 to 6 in favor of the wrong bettor.
- 6 or 8 (five ways): odds 6 to 5 in favor of the wrong bettor.

Again, there are good and bad points to each. You have to decide which one you are most comfortable with. Don't forget to watch for trends at the table. Since we're talking don't betting right now, the next couple of sections will go over some very simple systems to make you aware of how to start off.

Simple Don't Pass

Okay, you've decided to play don't on this particular day. You enter the casino, chart the tables, and find a game that is decidedly in favor of the wrong bettor. Perfect.

You buy in for $100 and wait for a new game to begin where you can place $5 on the don't pass. On the come-out roll, 7 or 11 means you lose; 2 or 3, you win the amount of your bet; 4, 5, 6, 8, 9 or 10, they become the point and the odds are in your favor. Twelve on the come-out roll is a push (tie) for the wrong bettor.

The shooter rolls and 6 becomes the point—not a great number for the don't bettor, but at least you have a 6 to 5 edge going for you. You can stop there and not make another bet, waiting for a decision on either the 6 to be thrown, in which case you would lose, or the 7 to be thrown, in which case you would win.

That shooter can throw for three weeks (don't worry, he won't) and pop out any number but the 6 or 7, and you're still alive. No other number affects that bet, except the 6 or 7. With a bet on the pass line, the right bettor cannot remove his bet because it is considered a "contract bet." That's because after a point is set, the house has a 6 to 5, 6 to 4, or 6 to 3 edge over any number that is the point.

If you're betting wrong, however, and the shooter establishes a number, the don't bettor has the edge and can remove his bet at any time. The house allows you to do this because the odds are now against them, as the don't bettor owns the edge with the 7.

There are don't bettors who take down their don't pass bet when it becomes a 6 or 8 because they claim, "It is an easy number to make, so I'll wait for a tougher one." They're dorks! The fact that they beat the 7 and have a 6 to 5 edge against that 6 or 8 is a plus in their favor. *Never* take down a don't bet—period! If you're afraid of the no-6 or no-8, simply place it and nullify it. Look at the following example:

Suppose you're betting $10 don't pass and the 8 becomes the point. You're worried that the 8 is easy to make. You still have that 6 to 5 edge, but if you're still worried, place the 8 for $6.

- If the 8 shows, you lose the $10 don't bet but win $7 or the place 8. You're only out $3.
- If the 7 shows, you lose $6 on the place 8 but win $10 for the no-8. You're up $4.
- Since you have six ways to win $4 and five ways to lose $3, you have put yourself in a great position. It's called hedging.

Go back to the simple don't pass method. You can sit with that initial don't pass bet and wait for the 7, or you could lay odds against the 8, as a lot of don't bettors like to do. I disagree. Why lay $6 to win

$5 when you already have $5 to win $5 and the odds are in your favor with the 7? My suggestion is, just stick with your naked don't pass bet.

Let's summarize the simple don't pass:

- Put $5 on the don't pass line.
- 7 or 11: you lose.
- 2 or 3: you win.
- 12: you push (tie).
- You can either lay the true odds against that number as an additional bet or you can just sit with your single bet on the don't pass.
- 4, 5, 6, 8, 9, or 10 is the point and the game has begun. You now have the 7 in your corner.
- Unless you want to establish an additional don't bet by coming through the don't come, I suggest no odds. (See the next section.)

Two Don't Numbers

Some don't bettors like additional numbers going for them, just like right bettors like multiple plays. Let's say 8 becomes your don't number and you wanna get a harder number to work for you. To pick up a "lay" against any number, you gotta lay enough money to win four units, plus 5 percent, plus laying the true odds. That means a player must lay out:

- $41 on no-10 or no-4. That's $40 to win $20, plus the $1 charge to make that bet.
- $31 on no-9 or no-5. That's $30 to win $20, plus the $1 charge to make that bet.
- $25 on no-6 or no-8. That's $24 to win $20, plus the $1 charge to make that bet.

A lot of players don't like to lay out that amount, even though they don't have to buck the 7 on the come-out. They can get another number by going through the don't come. You'll see this box in the upper-right-hand corner of the layout on both sides of the table.

Okay, you have $5 on the don't pass with 8 as the point. Lay odds of $6 against that point and put $5 in the don't come.

- If a 7 shows, you lose that $5 don't come bet but win $10 for your don't pass bet with odds.
- If 11 shows, you lose your don't come bet.
- If 12 shows, you have a tie. No bet.
- If 2 or 3 shows, you win $5 on don't come.
- If 8 (or whatever the point is) shows, you lose the don't pass bet with odds, the dealer places your don't come behind the 8, and you've reestablished the 8 as a don't bet.
- If 4, 5, 6, 9, or 10 shows, the dealer moves your don't come bet behind that number and you have two "no" bets.

The reason you laid odds against the don't pass bet was to protect yourself in the event a 7 showed. Then you'd be sure of getting a profit. (See the first example above.)

Once you establish the second don't bet (we'll say it was a 9), remove the odds off of the don't pass bet because you don't need them anymore, and I personally don't like laying odds, except to protect a don't come bet. Here's what you have:

- $5 don't pass: no-8.
- $5 don't come: no-9.

You can either sit with these two don't numbers or go through the don't come again to pick up a third don't number. You do *not* have to lay odds to protect your next $5 don't come bet, because if the 7 shows you lose the $5 don't come bet but win $10 for your no-8 and no-9. My suggestion? Glad you asked. If I have a no-6 and no-8, I'll go through the don't come to get a harder number like 4, 5, 9, or 10. If my first two don't bets are a combination of the 4, 5, 9, or 10, I'll sit with these two big edges going for me. If I have one hard and one easy, like the 8 and 9, I'll go back to get a third number, but even if it turns out to be a 6, I'll stop.

A summary:

1. You establish a don't pass bet and want additional don't numbers.
2. Lay single odds against the don't pass bet and put $5 in the don't come. Seven cannot hurt you.
3. When you establish the second don't bet, immediately remove the odds from the don't pass bet.
4. If you have two strong don't bets (4, 5, 9, or 10), just sit with them.
5. If you have a no-6 or no-8, just go through the don't come again to get better don't numbers.

IMPORTANT NOTE: If the shooter makes one of your don't numbers, go back through the don't come to get another, but—and I insist on this—only replace twice! don't get caught fighting a hot shooter. There will be another game coming up. (Reread and absorb that last paragraph.)

SECOND IMPORTANT NOTE: Don't go scratching your head, trying to decide why I didn't give you more information on lay bets. It's an aggressive although powerful play by don't bettors, but not appropriate for a beginner's book like this one. You dedicated wrong bettors will pick up this play down the road.

Betting Control on Don't

The don't bettor fears the hot roll where some shooter bangs out number after number knocking out don't pass and don't come bets.

How do you stop this? Simple, you use discipline, something that most gamblers lack.

To make my point, I'll have to give you a repeat quiz: Give me a number between 1 and 3. This should be a little easier than giving me one between 2 and 4, which most of you flopped. Okay, I heard a 2 somewhere out there. Keep that number locked in your mind; it's going to become a discipline tool.

Suppose you establish a 9 on the don't pass and a 6 on the don't come. You go for another don't come and get a 10. You smile confidently. The shooter pops the 10 on you and you go through the don't come again. This time, he gives you a no-4. You're back again with three don't bets!

Then he bangs the 4 on you, and chills run up and down your spine: This could be the start of something bad. You go through the don't come again and a 5 shows as another don't number. Again you're sitting with three don't numbers, but just as you are planning a trip to Hawaii with your winnings, the shooter throws a 5. Down goes your no-5.

That's it. Only replace *twice*, which you already have. Don't let one hot roll wipe you out. You're still sitting with no-9 and no-6, but that's all you want for this potential blockbuster roll. After you established your don't pass (9) and your don't come numbers (6, 10, 4, and 5), the shooter got hot and in the course of his roll, pulled down your 10, which you replaced with the 4 (which was also hit.) Then you came through the don't come a second time and got a no-5. The shooter promptly hit the 5, leaving you with only the no-9 and no-6. Stop right there. Only replace two times.

Many don't players go broke chasing bets with the idea that the shooter is due to seven-out. He isn't! The only thing "due" is my begging you: Do listen to me and do the right thing by cutting losses. You do this by not fighting a potential hot roll. Only replace twice.

Another thing, you're also due to listen to this suggestion about discipline: if that particular shooter bangs out your remaining don't pass and don't come, simply stand back and wait for the next shooter.

Replacing don't come numbers twice is enough. Also, when playing the don't pass line and a shooter beats you with two consecutive 7s or 11s on the come-out roll—back off! Let him continue his roll, but don't buck him!

Remember the two key numbers I mentioned in this chapter:

- *Three:* After you make your place bets, get a hit and regress to $6 on 6 and 8. Wait for *three* more rolls and then also take down that 6 and 8.
- *Two:* The maximum amount of don't pass or don't come numbers that you will replace when betting don't, when a potential hot shooter starts making numbers.

I'd give you more numbers to remember, but I don't wanna overload your think tank.

Simple Don't Hedge

I'm just gonna give you one simple don't hedge that you may like to look at. The intent in this book is to reach people who have no clue about craps, so sometimes I have to resist the temptation of going too deep. The "simple don't" has you making a don't pass line bet and just sitting with that dominant don't number. You've seen that system. It's in the section called "Simple Don't Pass."

The theory of getting multiple don't numbers into play has also been explained, but to repeat it:

- Bet the don't pass line, and after the point is established, lay odds against the point to protect your bet in the don't come, thereby having the 7 show you a profit if it appears.
- Get that first don't come bet into action and then remove the odds lay against the don't pass line bet.

These are two nice little conservative moves to get you started, but here is a simple hedge to get you to see the multiple moves that someday you will become aware of. Some quick reminders:

- Right bettors love having the 6 and 8 going for them.
- Wrong bettors love having the 4, 5, 9, or 10 working for them.

Let's say you're betting "wrong" and 5 becomes the point. You lay odds against the 5 and put $5 into the don't come. The shooter pops a 4. You have two great don't numbers (5 and 4). Now you can set up a nice hedge with a place bet of $6 on both the 6 and 8. (Don't forget to remove your odds off of the 5.) Look at the possibilities:

- If the 6 shows, you win $7. (Five ways to make a 6.)
- If the 8 shows, you win $7. (Five ways to make an 8.)
- If the 7 shows, you lose $12 on your 6 and 8 bet but win $10 for your no-4 and no-5. (Worst scenario: you lose $2.)

After the first hit on either the 6 or 8, you could take the $7 profit, remove the 6 and 8, and wait for a 7 to give you $10 more. Then even if the shooter bangs out both the 4 and 5 for a $10 loss, at least you already had a $7 profit. The potential dollar loss with the 7 is minimal ($2) and you have ten ways to win with the 6 and 8.

As the amount of your don't pass and don't come bets increase, the amount of your hedges get higher. The key is waiting for two hard (4, 5, 9, or 10) don't numbers to be set and then placing the 6 and 8. Take one hit, or even two if you feel aggressive, and then remove the place bets. If you place the 6 and 8, and one of the protection don't bets get made, remove the 6 and 8, and then reestablish a hard "no" number before replacing the 6 and 8.

One more suggestion: there is nothing wrong with having two hard don't numbers, placing the 6 and 8, and going through the don't come again. If a 6 or 8 is thrown, you'll win $7 at the same time you pick up another don't number. Then remove your place bets and just stay "wrong!"

What I'm driving home to you in a nutshell, is that you can bet both "wrong" and "right" at the same time. It's called hedge betting: you're hedging to cut your losses to the bone.

Wrapping Up Don't

I'm getting too deep for a beginner's book, so it's time to back off any additional moves that may confuse you. Go to my *Basic Craps* or *Advanced Craps* to see the load of offshoots for hedging and don't betting. Remember, it is not my intent to sway you one way or the other as to whether to bet right or wrong. In all of my books and tapes, my full intention is to get you to bet the correct way, which is one that adheres to money management, regardless of whether you are a right or wrong bettor.

Whether you play right or wrong, I want you to play correctly, and there is an incorrect way for both bettors. It is just as easy to play incorrectly when betting wrong as it is to play incorrectly when betting right. Look back over my approach to craps and notice that the message is geared to accepting small returns.

I gave you very simple approaches to start you off. Now it's up to you to go to the table. If you wanna bet wrong, be sure you bet wrong the "right" way.

All right, enough nonsense. Let's summarize the don't.

- Only go to cold tables.
- Leave the table if two consecutive shooters establish a point and then throw a minimum of six inside numbers—that table is too hot.
- Back off of a shooter who opens his roll with two straight naturals (7 and 11).
- Only lay odds to protect a don't come bet.
- When you have two don't numbers in place, only replace *twice*.
- When betting $10 or higher on either the don't pass or don't come and 6 or 8 becomes your number, offset with a hedge

place bet. That bet, in effect, becomes a wash.

- Finally, never let one shooter destroy you by constantly betting against him. If a shooter gets hot, just step back and wait for next one.

If you play smart as a wrong bettor, you can last a long, long time.

THE REALITY OF CRAPS

Right now, take a breather from the *ways* of betting to concentrate on the *whys* of betting. Here are a couple of questions that may be swirling around in your mind:

- Why is this guy concentrating so much on controlling money?
- Why is he not spending more time showing me how I can make double and triple the amount of my bankroll, so I can retire early?

Let's start with the first question. The reason I spend so much time telling you about money management and discipline is in case you still haven't grasped the reality of craps in particular, and gambling in general.

People have been gambling for years, just as I have. Am I rich? Heck no, but I know every single, solitary thing there is to know about gambling. So why aren't I rolling in dough? Because the reality of gambling is that no matter how smart you are, your chances of winning are never better than fifty-fifty. Did you hear that? Fifty-fifty is the best anyone can do. That's why I harp so much on looking for trends. I am the best player in the casino, yet my chances of winning are fifty-fifty. I learned this fact many years ago, just in time to save me from total destruction while looking for the big kill. The key was in controlling my money, cutting losses, and accepting small returns. That's why I stress money management.

Answer to the second question: Are you crazy? Looking for

double and triple the amount of your bankroll at a game that offers you only a fifty-fifty chance of winning? Suppose you placed the 6 as your only bet on the table. They pay you $7 to $6 for your wager, but there are six ways of losing and five ways of winning—the number of ways to make that 6 as opposed to the 7. Placing the 6 or 8 is considered a great bet in craps, and still the odds are against you. Unless you catch a streak, cut losses, and use money management and discipline, the odds are clearly stacked against you.

Is it possible to win? Of course! Will you lose all the time? No, but you got to leave tables where the trend is against you. Can you double and triple your starting bankroll? Occasionally, but not enough to offset the days when you get wiped out, looking for that bonanza. Should you use a conservative approach? If you want to win consistently at gambling, playing conservatively and accepting small returns are super-important.

Professional gamblers *know* the game they concentrate on and still they accept small but consistent returns. Dorks do *not* know the game they concentrate on and still go for big telephone-number returns. They eventually contribute to the building of bigger and better casinos. That's the reality of gambling.

SMART PLACE SYSTEM

Here is another chapter from *Advanced Craps*, whose message is fantastically powerful as it applies to the craps player.

We've just spent a lot of time going over the various moves in betting, and perhaps you're confused as to exactly which system you want to zero in on. That's going to be your choice. Over the years, you'll come up with different spin-offs of my theories, but there is one thing that will remain constant: the three key words to use at a craps table: "Take me down." The day you realize this is the day you become a player.

I ain't no high roller in a craps game and rarely ever get a big score, but they don't hang me out to dry because of those three magic words. Sure, I miss out on a lot of red-hot rolls, and sure I feel the eyes of the other players on me, looking at what they think is the chicken who just pulled back, but in my heart I know that it is the way to play. The times you miss out on a hot roll are more than made up for by the times you save bets. Yeah, you'll feel intimidated, but in the long run, it's the smart move.

Here's how I suggest you play, assuming you had a $440 session amount. Read on and absorb it:

1. Chart the tables to find one kicking off numbers.
2. Bypass the come-out roll.
3. After the point is established, play $44 inside.
4. After the first hit, take $14 and regress to $22 inside.
5. One more hit and off.
6. When you reach a profit of $150, change your starting amount.
7. Bypass the come-out.
8. Start with $66 inside.
9. After first hit, regress to $22 inside.
10. After second hit, come off.
11. When you reach a profit of $300, change the starting amount.
12. Bypass come-out.
13. After the point is established, place $88 inside.
14. After first hit, go to $44 inside.
15. After second hit, come off.
16. When you reach a profit of $450, change your starting series.
17. Bypass the come-out.
18. Place $120 inside.
19. After the first hit, regress to $66 inside.
20. After the second hit, regress to $44 inside or $22 inside (your option).
21. After the third hit, come off.

Keep increasing your starting series as you reach $150 plateaus. The amount you start with is based on your bankroll, but I've used $44 inside as a perfect start for 70 percent of the players in a casino. You'll notice I give you three hits when you get deep into a winning series. That is your option—you can stay with two hits if you like.

I don't know what you paid for this book, but it is worth one hundred times more than its cost if you follow everything I tell you, and this chapter is one of the granddaddys in terms of importance. Read and reread it over and over again. It contains the answer for you doubting Thomases who never believed that discipline is a big part of gambling. Will you pay attention to this advice and follow the suggestions in this chapter? I hope you do. Otherwise, it's a pity.

TWELVE-DOLLAR 6 AND 8

Let's wrap up the systems to use by giving you one that I believe everybody should adopt. It is based on the following truths:

- Most craps players like to bet "right."
- Most right players (90 percent) prefer the 6 and 8 as their place numbers.
- Most players in a casino have restricted bankrolls.

That last statement means that the average bankroll for 80 percent of all players is approximately $300. That is a lot of money in the real world, but small by the standards of playing tables with $5 minimums.

When you break that $300 into sessions, and you should—you know that by now—you have $100 to bring to battle. When you set a loss limit at 50 percent, as you also should, it's obvious you're restricted as to the moves you can make, but that happens to be the reality of gambling.

This powerful system, where the 6 and 8 become your right numbers 100 percent of the time, means that the amount of risk is only $24, and you need only one hit to put yourself in a no-lose situation. What else could you want? Here is the method you are already aware of:

1. Bypass the come-out roll.
2. Regardless of what the point becomes, place the 6 and 8 for $12 each.
3. Take one hit on either the 6 or 8, which would be $14, and regress both bets to $6 each.
4. Wait for three more rolls of the dice. If another 6 or 8 is not thrown, take down both bets.
5. If a 6 or 8 is thrown within three more rolls after the first hit, you'll have a $21 profit.
6. After the second hit, take down both bets and don't go back up until a new point is established.

If you can't grasp this simple, yet effective, system, it's time to go back to page one of this book and start over. You know all the pluses for this play, so let's go over the negatives:

- You aren't going to buy that yacht you had your heart set on from these winnings.
- You aren't going to retire at age twenty-six with a million dollars in the bank.
- You aren't going to be hailed as the most aggressive player who ever stepped up to a table.

Finally, a few reminders:

- Chart the tables to find a game kicking off 6s and 8s.
- Set loss limits (no more than 50 percent).
- Restrict your losing series to three in succession.
- Accept small returns.

If every single, solitary craps player in the world used this system in the casinos for one month, I wonder what the casinos would do. Try it, you'll see.

WRAPPING UP MONEY MANAGEMENT

Well, we bid farewell to the third part (but far and away the most dominant) of the Big Four. A car relies on many different things to be effective, such as a motor, oil, and gasoline. Each factor plays an important role in making that vehicle operate smoothly. If something breaks down, the car either stops or operates less than efficiently.

The same is true of the skills you must have when you play craps. Knowing the game is not enough, just like the motor in a car is important, but only one of a series of significant factors. I've listed some of the things we've touched on in this book. If any area needs reviewing, please leaf back and zero in on that subject. Here is what you need to do to be an efficient player:

1. Acquire a decent bankroll.
2. Predetermine right or wrong betting.
3. Chart the tables.
4. Break your bankroll into sessions.
5. Go to the lowest minimum table.
6. Decide on a method of play (hit and down, twenty-two inside, etc.).
7. Use the regression system.
8. Set win goals.
9. Set loss limits.
10. Accept small returns.
11. Set loss limits. (Oops, I already said that.)
12. Memorize the three key words: "Take me down."
13. Use guarantee and excess.

When you have all of the above safely tucked into your game play, then you can move to the final part of the Big Four! You know what it is, even though you may need time to develop it: discipline.

Question: What is money management?

Answer: Money management is knowing what to bet after a win and what to bet after a loss.

The series should be predetermined and followed to a "T." Let's go on to discipline and set up some more moves for you.

5

Discipline

WHAT IS DISCIPLINE?

Here we are at the final stages of the Big Four, and the biggest move that practically everyone is aware of but can't seem to incorporate into their play. Discipline in gambling is the art of being able to set win goals and loss limits and to strictly abide by these rules:

- Set an intelligent win goal of 20 to 30 percent.
- Set a solid loss limit of 50 percent or three straight losses.

The first part is easy. The next part is tough: stick to them! Get yourself to follow these percentages even when you're involved in a fast-paced game, with chips being passed back and forth, your watch saying it is not yet time to leave, and your heart pounding in anticipation of that big score. All restraint then goes out the window. I know, I've been there.

Discipline is easy to say, simple to understand, but so difficult to practice, yet this is what destroys all bettors in the casino. The casinos have discipline. You'll notice the maximum limits they place on their tables. You'll see the color-coded cards on the table denoting minimum and maximum bets:

White $2 card: max is $200.
Red $5 card: max is $500.
Yellow $10 card: max is $1,000.
Green $25 card: max is $2,000.

In some casinos, the color codes may differ, but the maximum bets allowed are put there to restrain a single player from breaking the house. That's smart on their part, and it is called discipline. Sure, they'll change that max for certain players, but only with confirmation from the pit boss.

Discipline is not only reaching a certain win goal and quitting: it is having the brains and guts to restrict losses. Why did I give you that test when I asked you for a number between 2 and 4? To indicate that three is the limit of consecutive games you can lose to signal your exit from the table. Not four, five, or six straight losses—three. That's discipline.

Many players don't have the brains to realize that when they lose a certain number of hands or rolls, the "due to win" factor is *not* going to kick in and give them a victory. I've had many players come up to me laughing, saying, "You're not gonna believe this. I just lost on eleven straight shooters. Can you believe that?" I usually answer, "Yeah, I can believe it, but I can't believe someone would be dumb enough to stand there and lose that many rolls."

The dork doesn't have a clue as to how to use discipline, even though he knows better. You can go back and read, memorize, and agree with all the things I've said throughout this book, but if you can't or won't put discipline into your arsenal, then the rest means nothing. Discipline. Get it or quit gambling.

PRESSING THE BET

In the last chapter, "Odds and Ends," you'll find a glossary of terms for the craps player, but for now I want to go over something called "press it." When you play craps, there will be loads of people at the table who believe in increasing their bets. In order to do this, they say, "Press it."

Simply put, it means "press up my bet." Let's say you have $6 on the 6 and 8 and the shooter pops an 8. There are several verbal responses to use:

"Same bet": Give me my $7 profit and leave the same bet there.
"Take me down": Give me my $7 profit and take my place bets off.
"Press It": Press (increase) my $6 place 6 to $12.

Let's suppose you had $12 place bets on both the 6 and 8. The shooter throws a 6 ($14 profit). Here are some of the comments you'll hear that player make to the dealer:

"Press up both bets": Add $6 to both the 6 and the 8.
"Press up the six": Add $12 to the place 6 bet. (The 8 stays at $12; the 6 is "pressed" up to $24.)
"Press one unit": You increase (press) the 6 to $18 and take back $8 of the $14 win.

People love to say "Press it!" It makes them sound like a big shot as their chips pile up on the numbers. The above three moves all revolved around increasing or pressing the place bets when the 6 hits. I do not agree with any of them for the first win, but you'll hear these things at the table.

My friend, Imus Pressit, is the biggest dork of all. He loves to let his bets increase. Here is one of his typical plays. Starting with $18 on the 6 and 8, Imus catches a hot roll:

1. The shooter throws a 6: "Press the 6 for $18." (Now he has $36 on the 6).
2. The shooter throws another 6 worth $42: "Press the 6 up to $60 and press the 8 up to $36."
3. The shooter throws an 8, worth $42: "Press the 8 up to $78, and here's $18 to press the 6 to $78." (He takes $18 from his rack.)
4. The shooter throws another 6 worth $91: Imus Pressit screams loud enough to be heard on the fourth floor of the parking lot, "Press the 6 and 8 up to $120 each. Press all my hard ways to $15, and here are some more chips. Place the 5 and 9 for $25 each. (He drops a handful of chips on the table.)

Naturally, he is on a roll and looks for the glances of the floor people to build up his bloated ego. While he is stretching his arm to pat himself on the back, the shooter throws the dice and the stick man announces, "Out 7, line way. Take the do's and pay the don'ts."

You'd think Imus Pressit was shot—four beautiful 6s and 8s back to back, and all he has to show for it is a losing roll. He not only lost his starting place bets but the profits and the extra chips he invested. He turns to anyone who will listen and cries, "I was just gonna take them down, I mean it." No, he wasn't. Guys and gals like Imus Pressit are dorks. They could wrap up pretty profits, but they throw it all away in hopes of the big score. They will never listen. You'll see Imus Pressit at many tables in all casinos. Don't laugh at him, though—he could be you.

DO YOU WANT DISCIPLINE?

Ask yourself the question that begins this section and see if you want to gamble:

- For fun
- For excitement

- As an outlet
- For entertainment
- For prestige
- To win money

The first five reasons don't require any thinking. You just saunter up to a table, buy in, and let it all hang out. Win or lose, you'll be laughing and clowning around with all of the people at the table who have the same perception of gambling.

Of course the ride home is a bummer, because you blew $600 even though you were ahead several times throughout the day. Naturally, you gave back the profit, plus what you started with, plus the money you borrowed from your wife, plus the money you found on the floor of the casino, plus the coins you found around the slot machines. You're in a rotten mood because you lost, and when you finally come out of your self-induced funk, you declare to your wife in all your infinite stupidity: "Well I lost my whole bankroll, but I sure had a good time today. I met a bunch of swell guys and we're all gonna meet at the bank tomorrow to get a second mortgage on our houses so we can do it again."

That's why we have gun laws—to protect women from shooting their lesser halves who make stupid statements like that. Maybe you are like this imbecile and don't really want discipline. It isn't easy to keep a harness on your emotions in a casino. You see all those chips and know they will never be yours if you play with control and discipline. The choice is yours. You can be a jerk and put your money at risk or you can use discipline and cut your losses to the bone. I know which way is right. Do you?

WHO IS DISCIPLINED?

Not many people. Sure, a lot of you will make promises that require discipline: to quit after a small profit, to cut losses, to brush your teeth three times a day, to lose weight, to quit smoking. They all take discipline.

As much as we *want* discipline, though, we realize we don't have it. We realize the work it takes to apply it. You're not alone in your inability to apply discipline to gambling—no matter how essential you know it is. The professional gambler has discipline, and he better. Three or four weeks of stupid, ill-advised moves that lack money management will drive him to the employment classifieds.

As I write this chapter on a rainy, cool morning in January, I find myself coming off of three consecutive losing nights in betting basketball. After a terrific weekend of picking the winners in three of the four Sunday games and zeroing in on three of the four under/overs, I dropped into a slump on Monday. It continued Tuesday and Wednesday. I'll bet tonight, but it will be a small one in order to right myself. If I lose, then tomorrow I'll reduce the bets even lower, until I reach a winning streak. That's the key: when winning, bet high; when losing, bet low. That's not too hard to remember and put into practice.

Who has discipline? Smart gamblers who want to win. Are you one?

SMART PERCENTAGE RETURNS

I know you wanna win a lot of money. We all do. We all look at gambling as the stepping stone to changing our lives. It's a great way to dream, but usually turns into a nightmare when the bubble bursts and we leave the casino frustrated and broke. Every day, people at casinos come over and tell me that they only want to double their money, or a guy with $300 says he'll be satisfied winning $1,000. Oh,is that all? They don't get it. When I tell them how far-fetched that goal is, they tell me it isn't worth it to go to the casino with $500 and play for a 10 percent return of $50.

Let me give you an example that you might identify with. Suppose you took $300 to the casino, and I told you to shoot for a 10 percent profit. You'd laugh, right? I ask people if they ever get ahead $30 with $300 and most say, "Yes, it's easy to get ahead 10 percent, but that isn't enough, so I go for more and usually end up losing." Exactly. If I ask them if it is easy to win 10 percent, the overwhelming majority says yes! Okay, hold that thought: it's easy to win 10 percent.

If it's so easy to win $30 with $300, why not take $3,000 and go for $300? That's only 10 percent. Or take $30,000, shoot for the same 10 percent, and you'll have $3,000 for the day. I think some of us could live on $3,000 a day, and it's the exact same percentage of 10 percent that you scoffed at, based on a $300 stake.

Let's go even further. Take the $30,000, but only go for a 5 percent return, which is 50 percent lower than the 10 percent you tell me is so easy to win. You'll still end up with $1,500 a day, a nice piece of change to give your wife—and maybe get you out of the doghouse you've been in from the last time you lost at the casinos.

Naturally, the problem is that you don't have big bankrolls to bring to battle, and I am not mocking you for that. I am mocking you for turning up your nose at the same percentage return that you would accept if you had a larger bankroll. The percentage is decent if you have the bankroll, and way back in the beginning I told you what the Big Four is. Right on top was bankroll. If you have a short bankroll, it is just as smart to take that 10 percent, or even 5 percent. If you can't accept that, then wait until you are well-heeled before you venture up to the tables again.

What's a smart percentage return? I say 10 percent. If you have a short bankroll, go for 20 percent, but be sure you set and follow the rules. A smart percentage return is a small percentage return. Someday, you'll realize what I'm saying is true. You'll think I walk on water. I do—but that's another story.

THE LAST CHIP

I ain't gonna spend a lot of time on this because you'll see yourself or someone you know standing out like a sore thumb when you see the comparison. My friend, I. M. Madork, tells me he has discipline. I always get excited and happy when I find someone who has control in the casino and am anxious to hear what they do.

I. M. Madork proudly tells me he only takes an amount of money he can afford to lose—say $500—and plays until it's all gone. I ask him, "Where is the discipline?" He says, "Oh, the discipline is when I go broke, I don't take extra money from a credit card or borrow from my wife and friends." He thinks that's discipline.

First of all, how can anyone, even this simpleminded idiot, say that they take money they can *afford* to lose?! He can't afford it. Can you afford to lose $300, or $500, or $1,000 without feeling the slightest pangs of guilt and anguish? This stupid habit of not setting loss limits on your bankroll or session money is idiotic. Let's say he goes up to a table with a $100 buy-in. The trend goes against him, and he's out $85 in a matter of four or five rolls. He makes a $5 pass line bet, takes $5 odds on the ten, borrows $11 from his poor unsuspecting wife, places the 6 and 8 for $6 each, and puts a buck on each of the four hard way numbers.

The shooter throws an 8 and he presses it. The shooter throws a 6 and he presses that, plus takes another $5 odds on the 10. The shooter sevens-out and he tells his wife, "Hey, I have discipline. I'm done. It took them almost twenty minutes to wipe me out, but they're not getting any more."

That's discipline? Did that boob think that those last few chips were gonna recuperate all his losses? Why did he bet down to those last few chips? Did he think he was going to hit a bonanza? Sure, and Miss World is waiting for me in my car. I'm a bigger dreamer than he is—and he's nuts. Set loss limits!

ACCEPTING YOUR GOAL

It doesn't take a strong person to set a disciplined goal for something they wish to achieve. The trick is sticking to that goal.

My friend, Lotta Fatt, is kinda chunky, if you consider the fact that she is five-foot-four and weighs four hundred pounds. She decided that her bikini was a little too snug, so she announced that she had set a goal to lose 150 pounds. Lotta got a lotta encouragement from her peers, who gave her credit for setting that goal. The problem is that Lotta set the goal in 1982 but never follows her guidelines. So what's the point in making this goal if she isn't going to follow it? Lotta says, "Well, it's a start at least."

The same is true for all of you who set a win goal of 20 percent or 30 percent of your bankroll. When the profit level is reached, you ignore your goals and keep right on playing. The excuses you give are usually one of the following:

> "I've only been playing a short time. What else can I do until it's time to leave?"
> "I ordered a drink and decided to keep playing until it came."
> "There's a good-looking woman at this table, and I think she likes me."
> "Now that I'm in the casino, thirty percent doesn't seem like much."
> "I told my wife I'd meet her at this table, and she's late."

The reasons why you won't accept your goals are cock-and-bull stories. You look for excuses to allow yourself to continue to play.

Many nonprofessional gamblers play to play, rather than play to win. They claim it is an outlet from the real world and it gives them time to relax. Fine, if that's what you want to believe, but why are you reading chapters on money management and discipline if you won't or can't follow the rules? If you want to stop making excuses and start pocketing some profits:

1. Set win goals.
2. Set loss limits.
3. Follow them.

You have two choices:

1. Do what I say and see how great it feels to win small, consistent amounts and cut losses to the bone.
2. Don't do what I say and suffer the consequences.

You choose.

DISCIPLINE ON LOSING DAYS

I hear a lot of stupid statements regarding the art of discipline. One of the dumbest I already shared with you is: "I have discipline, because I only take money to the casino that I can afford to lose." My obvious question is: "How about when you're on a losing streak. When do you quit? The ridiculous response is always, "When all my chips are gone, I know it's a bad day, so I go home. That's my discipline." You know the scary thing about the person who mutters these idiotic statements? They really believe they've got a handle on discipline.

The psychological drain of losing everything is something I went through many times. So did a lot of people, until we realized that you don't have to lose everything to realize things are not going your way that day. Throughout this book you've heard me refer to loss limits more than win goals. That's because loss limits are more important. I don't feel bad if I win a great big $22 on a given day. Sure, I'd like it better if it was $2,200 or even $220, but the main thing is that I didn't lose. Remember this sentence and repeat it over and over: "Winning is not as important as not losing."

Suppose I bring $1,000 to the casino. I'm not going to lose it all, so my loss limit kicks in at about 20 or 25 percent. I tell *you* to set a loss limit of 50 percent, but that's the *max*, not the average. If I lose $250 of my $1,000, I don't feel good, but at least there's $750 left in my pocket for the next trip.

Discipline should be practiced not only on the days you get ahead and leave with some profit; it should also be used on the days you are losing.

Cut those losses!

THE PROFESSIONAL GAMBLER

Let's backtrack a bit. This book is entitled *Craps for the Clueless,* so it is obviously aimed at people who have rarely or never ventured up to a craps table for one of the following reasons:

- They are intimidated.
- They think that if they say the wrong thing, they will have screwed up the whole game.

Wrong! Wrong!

As for intimidation, by now you should realize that there is absolutely nothing to be intimidated about, since the game is so simple. Also, there is no way you can say the wrong thing at the table, especially if you follow the "hit and down" theory. This is all you say:

- "Twelve-dollar 6 and 8, please."
- After one hit: "Regress both bets to $6 each, please."
- "Take me down, please."

That's it. How can you say anything wrong when you only have seventeen words to remember? Don't worry.

I've tried to break the game down to the most basic explanations and hope that you realize how simple it is, but then when we slid over to the chapters on money management and discipline, I wanted you to approach the game with a pro's mentality:

- Treat the game like a job.
- Cut losses to the bone.
- Accept small returns.

That's the way a pro looks at the game, and yes, it takes all the "joy" out of gambling. Gambling, by itself however, should not be the joy. The gambling part should be taken seriously. When you do this, you win. *Winning* is the joyous part.

If you go to a casino, you'll have shows, music, restaurants, drinks, beautiful women, atmosphere, and all the other things from which to derive joy, and even though you may say you only want to gamble for fun, I believe that deep down inside, you'd like to leave the casino a winner, at least 60 percent of the time. My intention is to try and explain the game in simple terms and hope you'll see how easy it is. Then I'd like to see you use even a teensy tiny bit of the theory that the professional gambler uses: "Cut losses and accept small returns."

I've been gambling since the Edsel was the greatest flop of the auto world. I know what it's like to lose, because it was the only thing I was consistently good at. Then I learned about money management and discipline, just in time to avoid working for a living. The light came on in that tunnel of blackness that passes for my brain, and I started to win and enjoyed the feeling. You will too. I am not trying to make you a professional gambler—I just want you to think like one—and win like one: very conservatively.

WRAPPING UP DISCIPLINE

There is no end to the messages I could give you on discipline. Maybe you're just getting started in gambling in general and craps in particular. It doesn't matter. Someday, you'll realize that the advice I try to impart to you on money management and discipline will be the thing that will determine whether you win or lose.

You've heard me preach over and over about the importance of setting loss limits and win goals and accepting small returns. Breaking your bankroll into sessions, charting the tables, and playing only at games that are going in the direction you predetermined to play is a part of discipline. Leaving a table when you lose at three consecutive games or when you lose the amount of your loss limit are forms of discipline.

Let's say you set 40 percent as your loss limit (50 percent of your session money is the absolute maximum you can afford to lose) and you find yourself at a chopping table. Your chips are slowly being ground away, but you still haven't lost three shooters in a row or reached the 40 percent loss limit. Don't be a dork and stay there. Leave that table. I set loss limits but rarely ever reach them, and that's because at the first sign of the table going against my way of playing, I look to run.

We'll say my buy-in is $500 and I set a loss limit of 40 percent. After six or seven shooters, when I am playing $44 inside, the table becomes very choppy. Maybe I've only lost 20 percent of that $500, but that is totally irrelevant. The fact is that I am losing. I pick up my chips and wrap up that session. Why stay at a table that is not beneficial to me? There are plenty of others to choose from. So I start walking, looking for another table to chart. Maybe I'll catch a game where my chances of winning are better.

I know doggone well that many of you can't or won't listen to this advice because it is so restrictive to your idea of just "having fun." Well, can't you "have fun" at a table where you are winning a few dollars? Of course you can.

Personally, I don't look at gambling as fun. To me, it's a job and a tough one. Maybe you'll follow my suggestions on money management and discipline, and maybe you won't. That's your choice. Someday, however, you'll realize what it takes to win consistently. The word is discipline. The results are excellent.

6

Odds and Ends

This sixth and final chapter will tie together all the things that were explained in the first five. Every one of those points are significant to the overall approach to gambling. I stressed loss limits, which is focused on in the money management chapter.

Chapter 2 keyed in on protecting your bankroll by breaking it into sessions, thereby cutting down your chances of losing your whole stake at one table.

In Chapter 3, I dwelled on the layout, explaining all of the facets of the game, plus the object of craps in general. That chapter is important from the standpoint of grasping the theory of craps, but its impact on winning is less than the other three chapters on bankroll, money management, and discipline. So make sure you look at those three important chapters.

As you progress in your playing the game of craps, you'll come up with your own theories. That's good, because maybe your theories will work for you better than mine and will get you to your ultimate goal: winning money. The next few sections will touch on several things that may seem unimportant right now, but give them a chance and you'll see how they tie in.

TIPPING

TIPS: an acronym that means "to insure proper service." Tipping is a big part of our society, and we encounter it every day. Obviously, tipping is for services rendered, and it's hard to find a common ground for the exact protocol, because it is constantly changing.

In the casinos, the cocktail waitresses depend on tips because of their low base salary. The drinks are free, but these people really do contribute to an important part of your day in the casinos. So cocktail waitresses should be tipped. A fair tip is $1 per drink, which is what most patrons give out. You cheapskates who order drinks while you're playing and then stiff the women who bring them deserve the name, cheapskate. You earn it. Good grief, give her a break! You'd pay $5 for the same drink at a local bar—here you're getting it free.

The dealers themselves aren't going to retire on their base salary either, so they, too, rely on tips to make a decent take-home salary. Tipping the dealers isn't going to get them to cheat for you, but it does make them aware that you recognize their efforts, so they'll pay particular attention to your method of play.

My suggestion is not to tip when you leave the table, because then the dealer does not get the chance to help you at the game. That does not mean you should ask him or her how to play, but a sharp dealer picks up all players' methods and reminds them when they forget a move.

Let's say you are playing $22 inside, and after the first hit on the 5, 6, 8, or 9, you take down the 5 and 9. Maybe due to fatigue or the fact that you're checking out the cocktail waitresses, you forget to ask the dealer to take down the 5 and 9 after a hit. A sharp dealer will remind you.

A courteous dealer tends to make the game enjoyable and is obviously worthy of a tip. I always tip and have a pattern that seems fair. When I am winning, I'll play the hard ways for the dealers. Every five or six shooters (again, if I am winning), I'll toss $4 into the center of the table and tell the stick man, "Two-way hard six and eight." That means $1 hard 6 and 8 for me, and $1 hard 6 and 8 for the dealers. The hard way plays are not one-roll action bets, so the dealers get a longer look at their chips in action—and who the "generous" player is.

Playing the any craps or the yo (please call it 11 so you don't sound too much like a wise guy) means you've got the dealers involved strictly in a one-roll action bet. The chips aren't on display for very long, and I never really was an advocate of those high percentage one-rollers. Stick with the hard way plays.

The bottom line is: you should tip the cocktail waitresses and dealers, and I don't mean with dimes. Exception: a surly, unfriendly dealer or even one who is trying to break the speed record. These types are usually in blackjack and put a ton of pressure on the players. Remember what TIPS (to insure proper service) also means: good service means good tipping.

Use your own judgment in this area. You know my position.

PROPOSITION BETS

A final word on these bets, which offer tempting payoffs. The rewards are greater, but so are the risks. A favorite play at the table is the 11, which offers a payoff of 15 to 1. That means you will receive $15 for every buck you invest, and it is a one-roll wager.

Since there are thirty six combinations that could occur on every roll, we find that only two of them (5-6, 6-5) could result in an 11. The chances of eleven showing are thirty-four to 2, or 17 to 1. The casino pays 15 to 1. That's a big bite.

The any 12 (called box cars) and any 2 (called snake eyes) offer 30 to 1 payoffs and attract plays from people trying to catch up. Of the thirty-six combinations that could occur, only one roll (6-6) could result in a payoff for box cars. The true odds are 35 to 1, while the payoff is 30 to 1. Doesn't sound too inviting to me.

The any seven (called "Big Red") is the biggest sucker play of all. Again, it is a one-roll action wager, paying 4 to 1. There are six ways to make a 7 out of thirty six combinations. The real payoff should be 5 to 1. The casinos pay 4 to 1.

Do *not* play the any seven, even if you think it is a great hedge to play the don't pass, where the 7 on the come-out roll can beat you, and hedge it with an any seven. Although it sounds good, it lacks merit. You'll be ground to bits if you try it.

The next section dwells on the hard way bets and the terminology of the payoffs.

HARD WAYS AND "TO" AND "FOR"

No, I didn't misspell the *to* and *for*. The section title is correct. First of all, let's dispel the old-wive's tale that playing the hard ways is a sucker bet. It's not a tumble in the sand with Miss World, but it is not a knee in the groin, either.

When I go to the table, as I explained earlier, I bring an extra $20 over and above my session money. If I see a series of hard ways being thrown, I'll invest a couple of chips on the hard 6 and hard 8. I'll do this for three consecutive games, looking for that trend to continue. The most I'll lose is $6. If I win, I'll increase the hard 6 and hard 8 and start a play on both the hard 4 and hard 10. If I continue to win, I'll start increasing my bets on all the hard ways. If I lose three shooters in a row, I stop. This is simple to understand, although you might like to rearrange the numbers.

You already understand these moves, but I want to explain the difference in terminology between the tables in Atlantic City and in Las Vegas.

Suppose you bet $1 on the hard 6 in Atlantic City. The payoff reads 9 to 1. That means you get paid $9, and your $1 chip remains in action. You have $9 in your rack, and you can either leave your chip in action or take it down. You started with $1 and ended with $10, which results in a $9 profit.

In Las Vegas and many other casinos, the words on the hard 6 and hard 8 read: 10 for 1. They aren't giving away the ranch. If the hard 6 (or 8, or whatever you're playing) is hit, they give you back $9 plus the $1 bet from your hard way that hit. You still end up with $10, which results in a 9 to 1 payoff. If you want to go back up on the hard way for that hit, you have to toss a chip back into action. They look different in each place, but the payoffs are exactly the same. One pays 9 *to* 1, the other 10 *for* 1. The bottom line is that they both end up at the same amount.

Do I play the hard ways? You bet I do. Should you play the hard ways? It's up to you. The risk is small, and if and when you catch a little run, you can pick up some nice profits—if you follow the up and pull method: up your bets on all the hard ways and pull back a profit from each payoff, but be sure you pull back something, large or small.

CONTROLLED AGGRESSION

We may as well go over this move again, even though it may seem like I've beaten it to death. That's because it is so important. It has to do with accepting small profits after every hit on one of your place numbers.

This example is for a semiaggressive player to stay in action while holding down potential losses. My theory is to grab a few bucks for every winning roll. I'm gonna give you an example based on playing the 6 and 8, but realize right now that the drawback with the up and pull method in craps is that "sister" numbers work together. This means that when you increase a place number after a hit, the sister number gets the same increase.

- If the 6 hits, both the 6 and 8 should be decreased together.
- The same is true if the 8 hits.
- If the 5 hits, both the 5 and 9 should be decreased together.
- The same is true if the 9 hits.

The example will be used on the 6 and 8, even though it would have been simpler with the 5 and 9. We'll start with the $44 inside method and incorporate the regression before we get to the up and pull.

1. Bet $44 inside.
2. The 9 hits. You get paid $14 and regress to $6 on 6 and 8. You're in a no-lose situation.
3. The 6 hits and you get paid $7. I would *not* take a profit but instead want to go up to $12 on 6 and 8.
4. Add $5 from your rack to the $7 you won, and tell the dealer to increase your 6 and 8 to $12 each.
5. At this point, you have $12 on 6 and 8. Even if the shooter sevens-out, your total loss is only $3, although another hit on the six or eight gives you a $14 payoff. If you took both place bets off, your profit would be $35 with a $3 potential loss.
6. Go back to number four, where you went up to $12 on the 6 and 8. Suppose an 8 hits and you receive a $14 payoff. Place the 5 and 9 for $5 each and pull back $4.
7. You can remove all bets at any time, with a nice profit for this shooter, or you can continue.

(A quick note: This is a controlled aggressive series that has held down any possible heavy loss but has you sitting with four place bets that hasn't cost you diddly-squat.) There are so many ways of handling place bets that I could use up three hundred pages just giving you options and offshoots. To continue:

8. Suppose a 6 shows and you are paid $14. Here are options for you to choose from:

    a. Increase the 5 and 9 to $10 each and pull back $4.

    b. Increase the 6 and 8 to $18 each and pull back $2.

    c. Take the $14 and leave the same bets.

    d. Take $14 and regress the 6 and 8 to $6 each, giving you $22 inside.

    e. Take $14 and bring everything off, except $12 on the 6 and 8.

    f. Take $14 and bring everything off, except $6 on the 6 and 8.

Had enough options? Don't laugh. This is what you're gonna be up against, which is the reason I want you to determine your moves *before* you reach the table. It is also why I want you using the place numbers, in order to open up these various avenues of control.

This section was purposely put at the end of the book so that you could see all the moves that are open to you. I will repeat this message again: This book is *Craps for the Clueless*. By now, if you stayed with these messages, you are no longer clueless. I strongly urge you to graduate to my *Basic Craps* and to *Advanced Craps* and zero in on more moves.

To wrap up this series, I am not going to tell you which of the above seven options I would take. We're all different, and each person has to make his own decisions.

Don't forget: These options and more pop up after every single hit. Be ready.

My choice would have been...nope! I'm going to let you decide. There is absolutely no wrong choice. It's all up to each person's theory.

A "COMMERCIAL"

This is going to be short and to the point, even though it may come across as a commercial. I've written ten other books on all forms of gambling: blackjack, card-counting, sports handicapping, roulette, slots, and poker. My favorite is sports handicapping, but that's because it is my main source of income, along with poker. These are my two favorite gambling outlets (for want of a better word).

There is *Basic Craps,* which was my biggest seller until I released *Advanced Craps. Advanced Craps* is *the* book on gambling, due to its depth and insight into the money management moves. I've also made twenty-three videos on all the different games, so you can decide if any of them suit your fancy. In all my books and tapes I zero in on money management and discipline, so don't think the messages are different. The Big Four and Little Three are constants.

If you need assistance or wish to order these tapes, please write to me through my publisher, whose address is listed on the last page of this book.

INTIMIDATION

This is a favorite subject of mine because it touches so many people. We're all intimidated by something or other in our lives, and many times it prevents us from doing things we would like to.

Many years ago, while growing up in New Jersey, my early years were spent in the playground with my buddies, playing softball, basketball, football, honing my skills for the day when I'd be a star athlete. On the way home each night, I had to walk through some woods where there was a gang of older guys led by a bully about a year older than me, named Frank. I was terrified of Frank, because if any of us younger guys were caught, he'd beat us up and harass us. It got so bad that I stopped going to the playground, unfortunately missing out on many chances to play ball. After a couple of months, my dad, my best friend in the whole world, asked me what was wrong.

After days of hedging, I finally told him about the bully Frank and how I was scared to go near him. My dad told me that if I didn't meet this problem head on, I'd always be avoiding doing things I really wanted to do. He told me to have it out with Frank—in other words, fight him.

No way was I going to take that bully on! I'd only get creamed. My dad kept after me, even offering to go with me. I finally convinced myself to get it over with. I took my buddy, Irv, with me and went into the woods.

Frank came after us and starting punching my arm, over and over. I wanted to run and hide but just kept backing away. Irv yelled out, "Hit him! Hit him back!" Frank just laughed and repeated what Irv said, "Go ahead, yellow belly, hit me." I looked at him shaking his fists, threatening to belt me again. Finally, I swung my right hand and caught him right on the nose. Blood squirted all over both of us. I had never hit anyone before. What a feeling it was to see that person appear dumbfounded!

He grabbed his bleeding nose and screamed. I punched him in the stomach with a straight left and his knees buckled. He started to fall. I had a half-second to get in one more shot, a right to his left eye, and he went down like a sack of potatoes. It was over. I stood there, waiting for Frank to get up and pummel me. He didn't.

We never spoke again. I walked past him every day after that, coming home from the playground through the woods. I had been intimidated for years by someone who in the long run was preventing me from doing my thing. Yet there was absolutely no reason to be scared or intimidated by this situation.

My point is that we are intimidated by whatever we choose to be intimidated by—nothing or nobody can do it to us. We do it to ourselves until we say, "no more." The same is certainly true in the casino. You may be intimidated by the craps table and the seemingly fast action. You may be afraid to go up to the table, afraid someone will see you're a beginner. You may be afraid to take your bets down for fear the other players will criticize you. You may be afraid to hedge, take your bets off, regress your bets, all because you'll think someone will say you're cheap. The game of craps may absolutely intimidate you.

You're not alone. A lot of people play slots and video poker because they're afraid of the tables. There is *nothing* to be intimidated about. You probably now know more about the table than anyone.

Don't waste time worrying about things or being afraid. The story I told you is true. Frank was my intimidator as long as I let him be. It took me a long time to realize that I was in control.

Go in there and punch out those tables!

"LUCK" IN GAMBLING

Every day of every week of every month of every year (in other words, all the time), people tell me they have no "luck" in gambling. I ask them what happened, even though I've heard the story 37,681 times. Only the names of the people and the name of the casino change:

"If my bad luck was water, I'd drown to death."
"If I didn't have bad luck, I'd have no luck at all."
"God hates me. All he gives me is bad luck in the casino."
"My luck is so rotten, the casinos send limousines for me."
"I have rotten luck—I was up seven hundred dollars today and figured this was my big chance. Then bad luck set in and I lost the seven hundred dollars, plus the two hundred dollars I brought."

Stop the music! Stop the presses! Stop the crying! That last example sums up all of the dorks who get ahead and still can't or won't quit. A lot of times, people who start with $200 or $300, or even $100, get ahead three, four, or even five times the amount they started with. That happens many times because you will definitely catch hot streaks or hot trends in all games—but these trends don't last forever. You must set cues to get you to realize when things start going the other way. I use the number that sits between 2 and 4 and rhymes with flee. It means that when you lose three games in a row, it's time to *flee* the scene.

I. M. Madork just said: "Thirty-three rhymes with three. Why can't I wait for thirty-three straight losses before I quit?" And you wonder why they build stalls for donkeys?

You don't lose at gambling because of bad luck, just as sure as you don't win because of good luck. You win because you catch a trend, use money management, and use the up and pull strategy to take advantage of these streaks. You also, however, need to have the brains to quit when the trend starts going against you. You lose because:

- You don't have money management.
- You don't have discipline.
- You don't understand trends.
- You don't realize that you're playing at a game that offers you only a fifty-fifty chance of winning, even if you're a perfect player.
- You don't quit with small returns.
- You don't set loss limits.
- You don't set loss limits! (This must be important!)

In gambling, there ain't no such thing as luck—there are only dorks with no discipline!

A FINAL WORD ON REALITY

Well, if you understand the basic approach to craps and all the plays at the table, you've come a long way, but before you go nominating yourself for a Nobel Prize, just step back for a moment. Maybe you know *about* the game, but do you know what the game is all about? It's about cutting losses and accepting small returns. It seems to me that I've already said that, but sometimes you gotta say it six, seven, eight times before it reaches home.

The reality of gambling is that it's rough to win at, as shown by the hundreds of millions of dollars that the casinos make each year. I could tell you that if you follow all my suggestions, you'll be able to win so much money that you could build your own casino, but that would be untrue.

For laughs, go to a craps table and observe the other players. They live and die by every roll, never taking their bets down, never thinking of wrapping up some sort of profit, and they die a little when the shooter uncorks that 7—making even the strong ones weep. They don't get it. They don't get the reality of gambling. Remember: Even a perfect player has only a fifty-fifty shot (at best) of winning.

I've said it before, but you may as well swallow it one more time: It ain't how much you win that is important. It's how little you lose that counts!

That's reality.

Glossary of Terms

Buy Bet An opportunity for a player to "buy" either the 4 or 10 for a charge of 5 percent of the potential win. It reduces the edge against the player from 6.67 percent to 5 percent.

Charting Checking out a table to see if the dice are hot (throwing numbers) or cold (sevening-out).

Come Bet After the shooter establishes a point, players may put chips on the come and the next roll of the dice acts exactly as the pass line, establishing additional numbers.

Craps Any combination of 1-1, 1-2, or 6-6 that a shooter throws.

Do Bettor See right bettor.

Don't Bettor See wrong bettor

Don't Come Bet After the point is established and the player wishes to get additional don't numbers, the chips are put in the don't come box. The next roll affects that bet.

Don't Pass Line Area on a table where wrong or don't bettors place their bets.

Field Bet A one-roll action bet that a player can make anytime. He or she wins if the shooter throws a 2, 3, 4, 9, 10, 11, or 12 (double payoff). He or she loses on 5, 6, 7, or 8.

Hard Way A bet where a player wagers that the shooter will make the 4, 6, 8, or 10 hard. That would be 2-2, 3-3, 4-4, or 5-5. Any other combination of those numbers would be called "easy."

Loser A player who gets ahead and doesn't have the brains or guts to quit with some type of profit.

Natural A 7 or 11 thrown on the come-out roll in which the shooter is trying to establish a point.

Odds Pass line bets pay even money. Taking "odds" behind the pass line allows players to be paid true odds of making that number versus the number of ways to make the 7. (Example: true odds of making the 4 or 10 is 6 to 3. A \$5 odds bet pays true odds of 2 to 1.)

Pass Line   Area on a table where all do or right bettors place their bets.

Place Bets   Bets on 4, 5, 6, 8, 9, or 10 that the player has the opportunity to place at any time, without having that number show as a point.

Point   A number (4, 5, 6, 8, 9, or 10) that the shooter establishes as his point and must be made again before rolling a 7.

Push   A tie. No action. (Example: don't bettor puts \$5 on don't pass or don't come and 12 shows. It's a "push," or tie.

Right Bettor   A player who bets that the shooter will throw a lot of numbers before sevening-out.

Shooter   Every player at the table has the option of throwing the dice in turn. When that happens, the player who rolls is called the shooter.

Vigorish   A hidden percentage that the casino has going for them on every bet.

Winner   A player who knows how to get ahead and quit with profit, regardless of the amount.

Wrong Bettor   A player who bets against the shooter making his point.

Yo   Slang term for a bet on the 11. Pays 15 to 1.

THE ULTIMATE GOAL

Winning! That's what we all hope for. Yeah, I know there are people who play for fun, for excitement, as an outlet, and for other reasons, but the ultimate goal should be to leave that table with more money than you started with. On the days when you catch trends going against you, the smart move is to set loss limits and abide by them. Some of you will, a lot of you won't, but that's the way the ding dongs.

I hope you enjoyed this book—it's one of eleven so far. Each one is geared to money management and discipline and getting you to zero in on sensible "ultimate goals."